COLORING BOOK FOR ADULTS

Spectacular Animals & Mandalas

Slow Down & Relax with Art

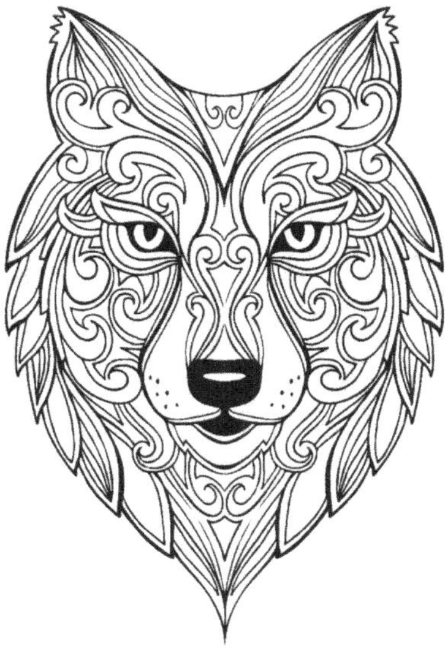

This Book Belongs To

____

____

____

Color Test

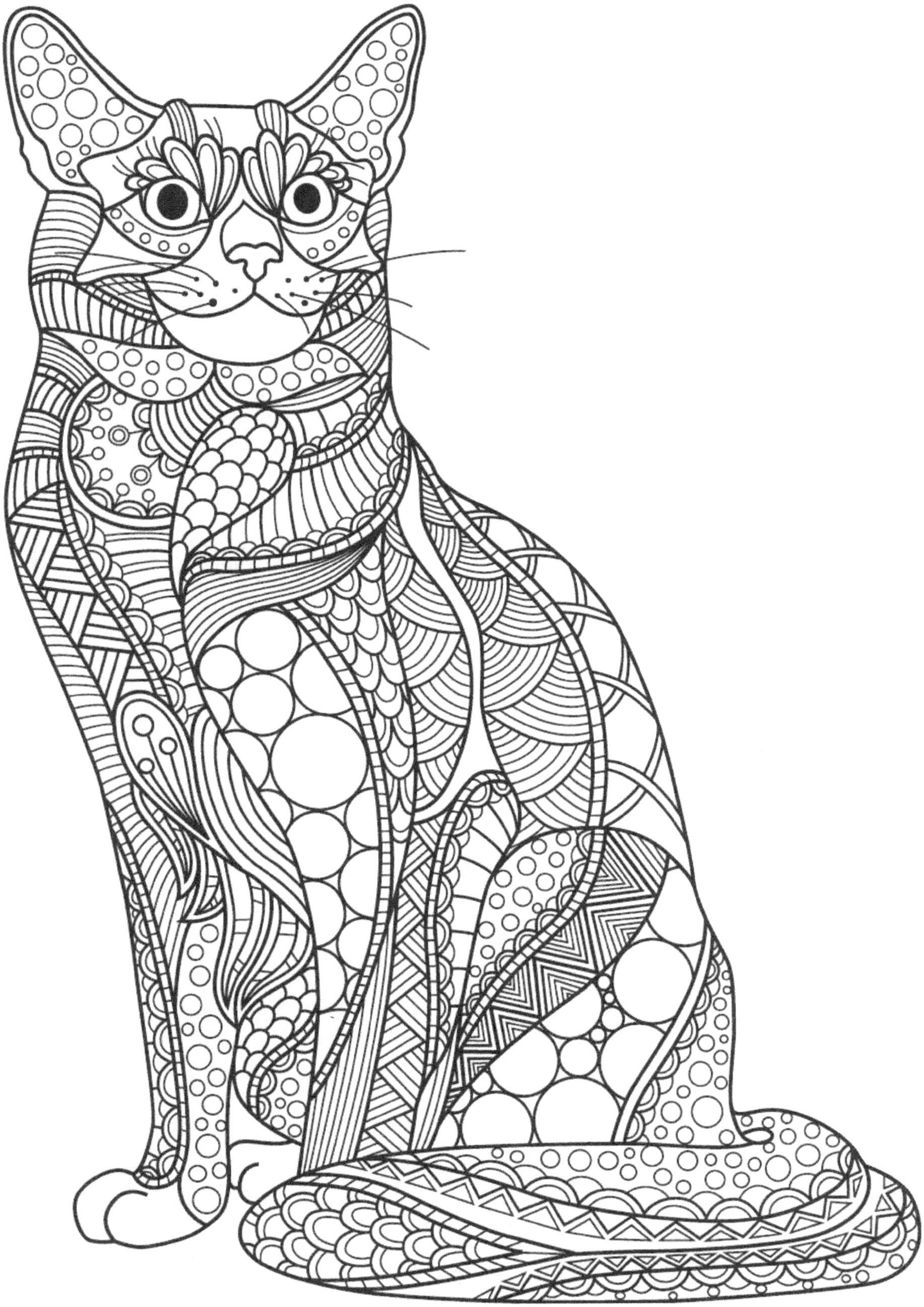

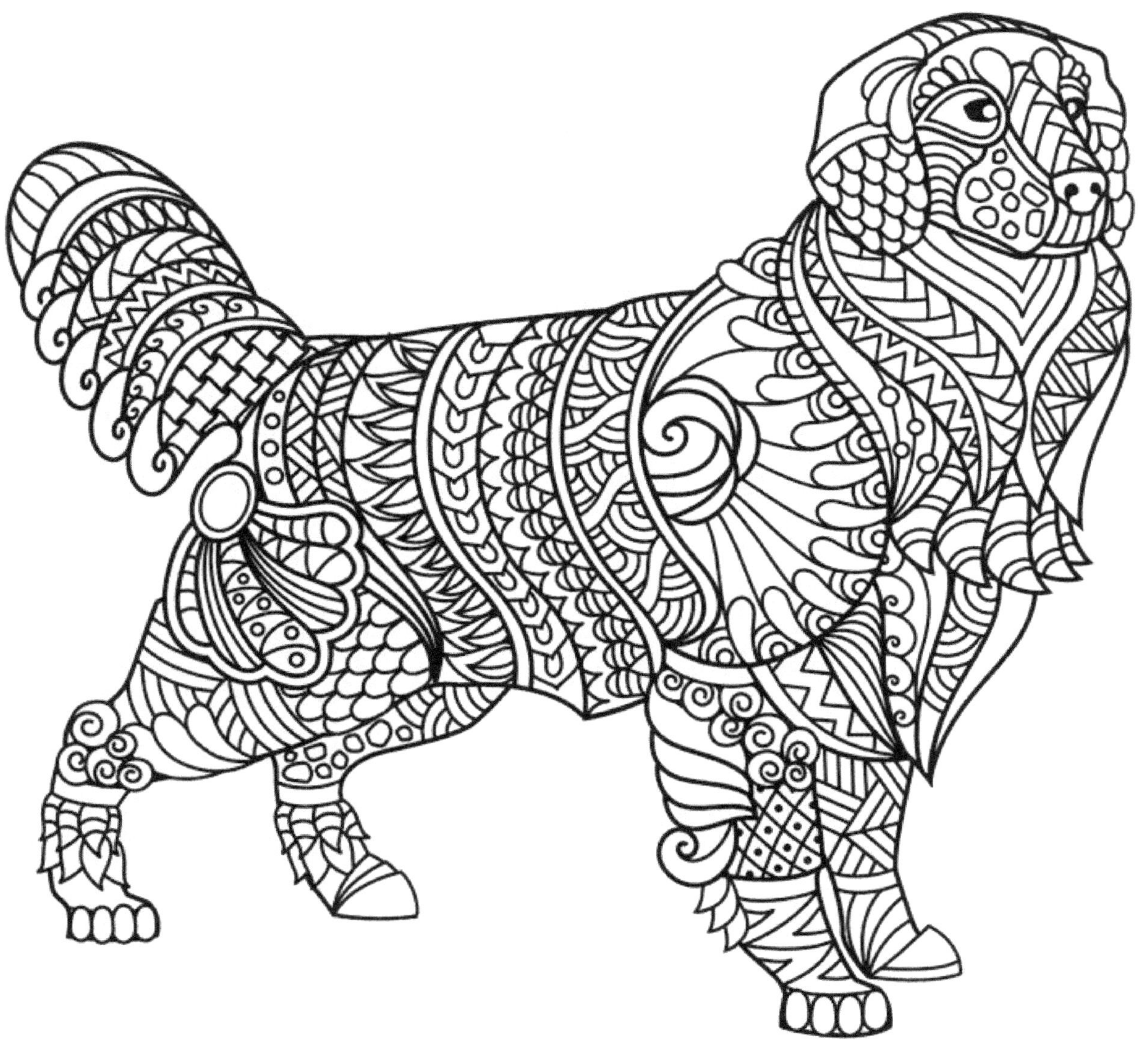

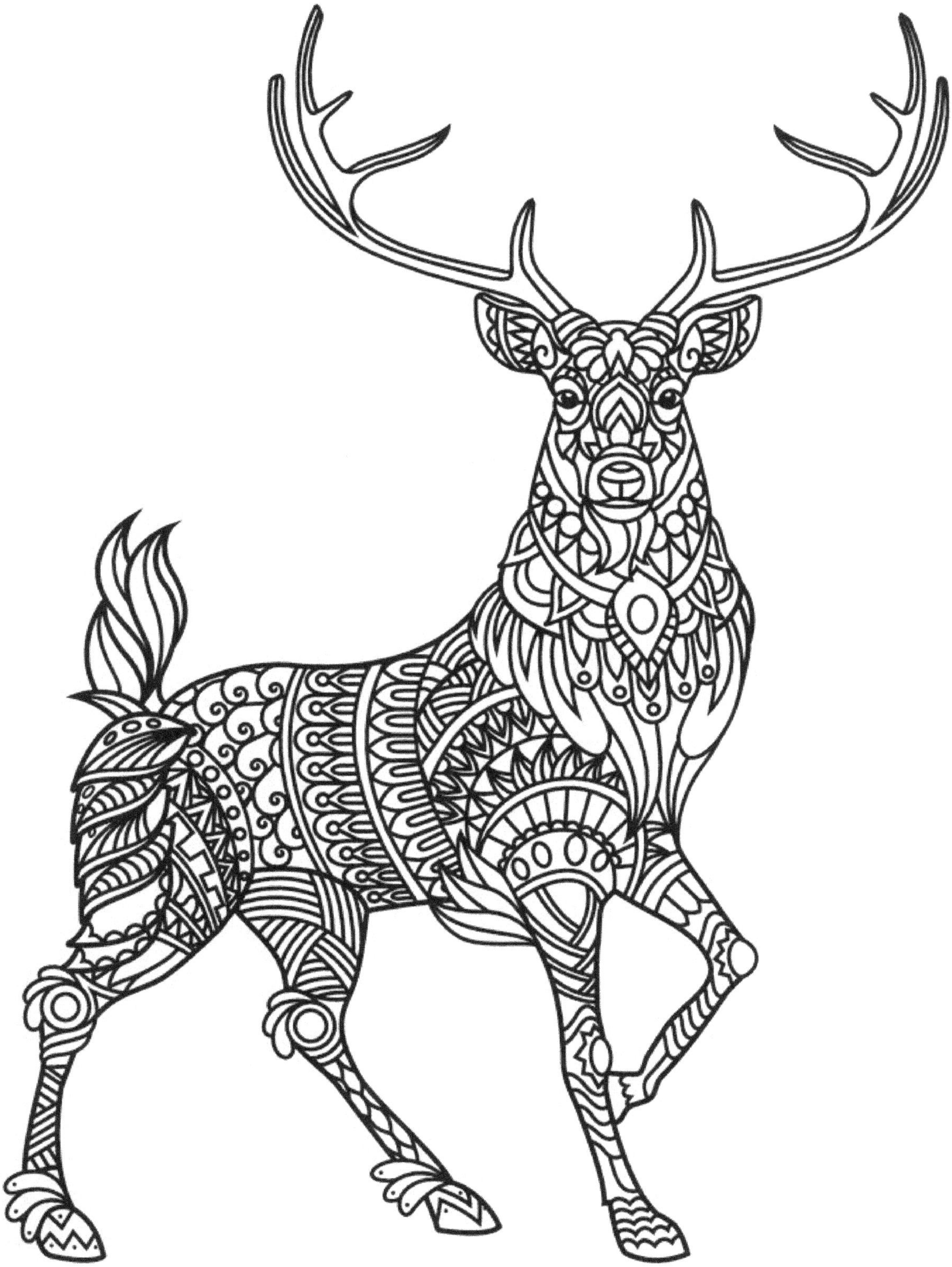

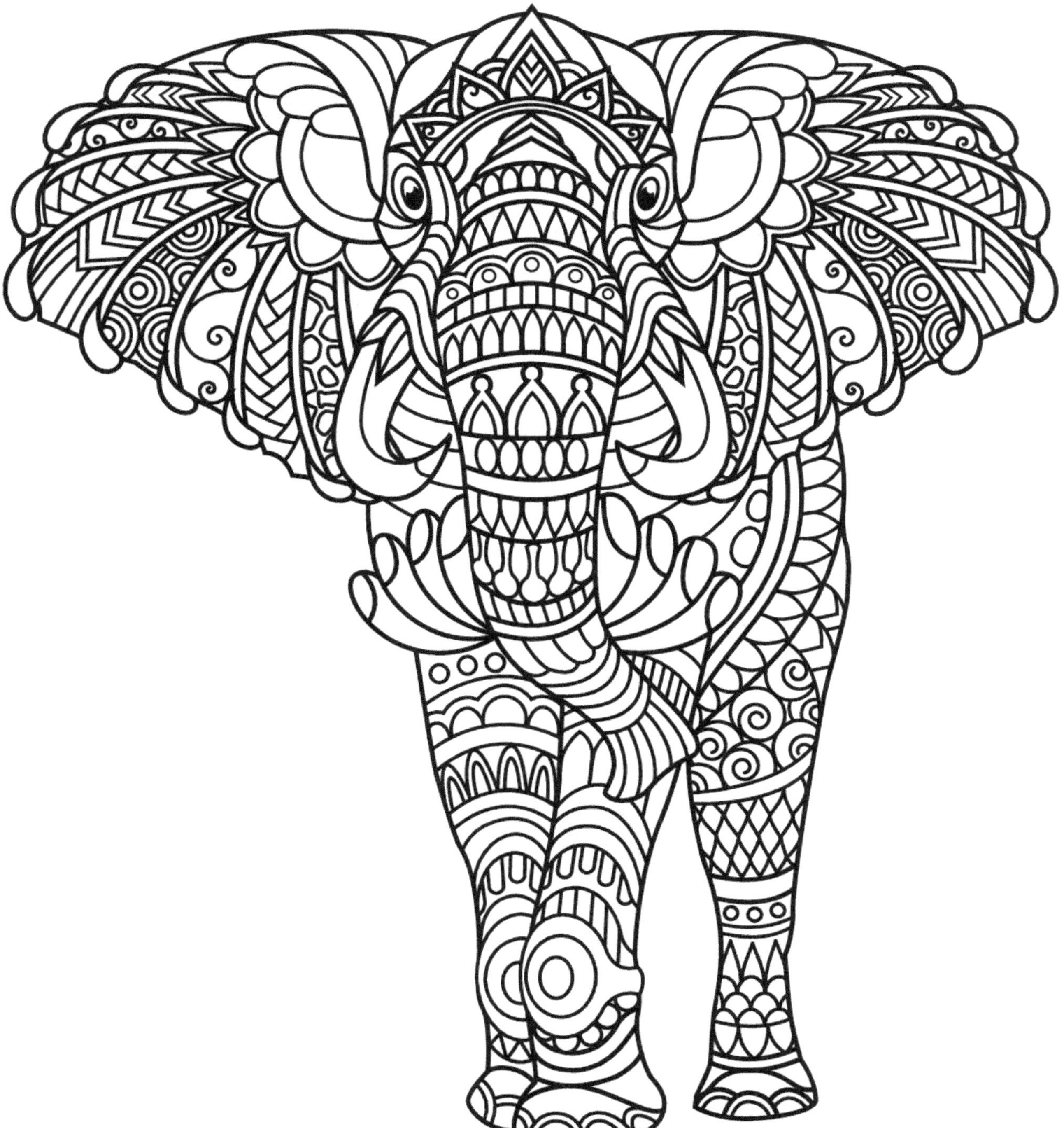

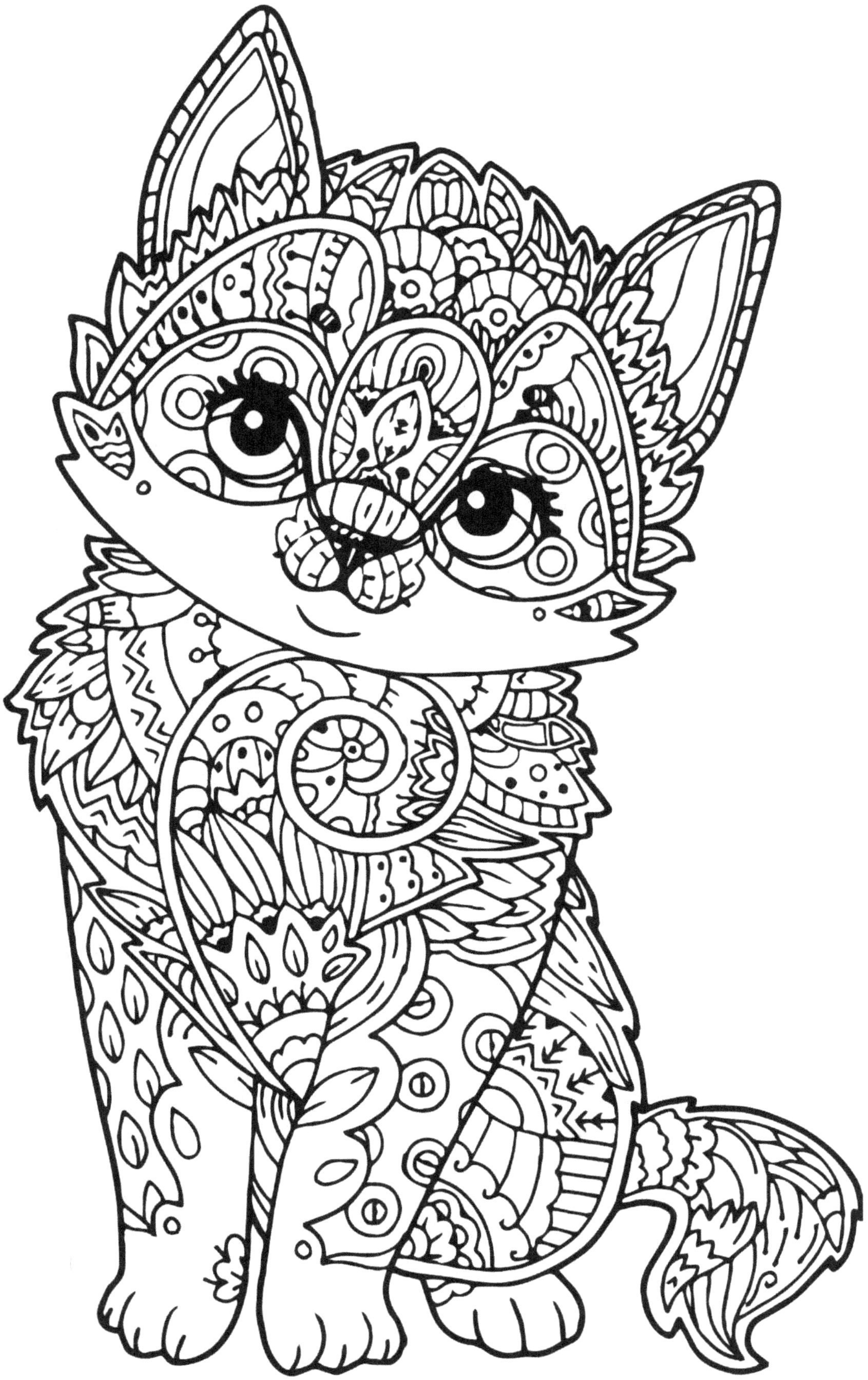

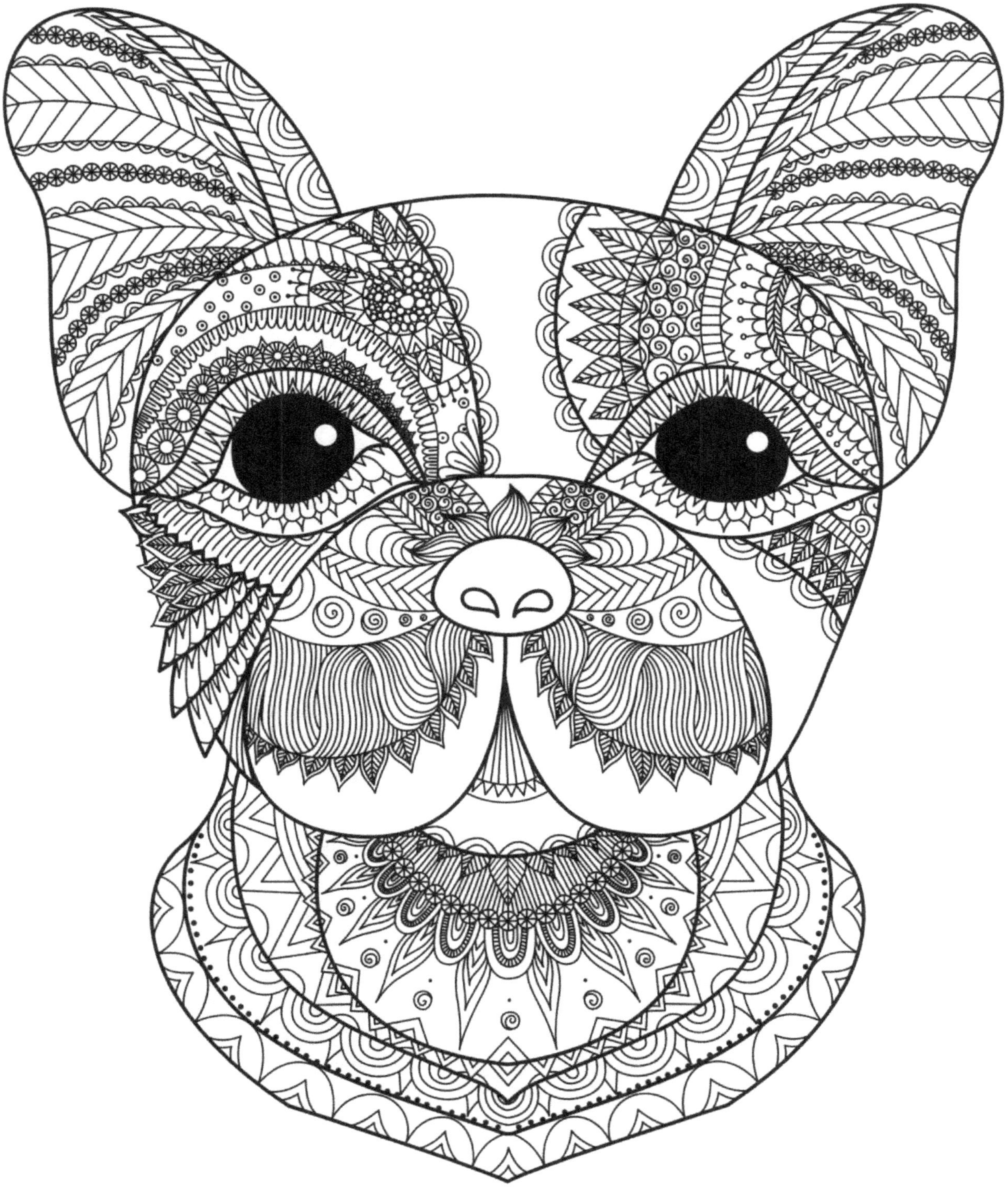

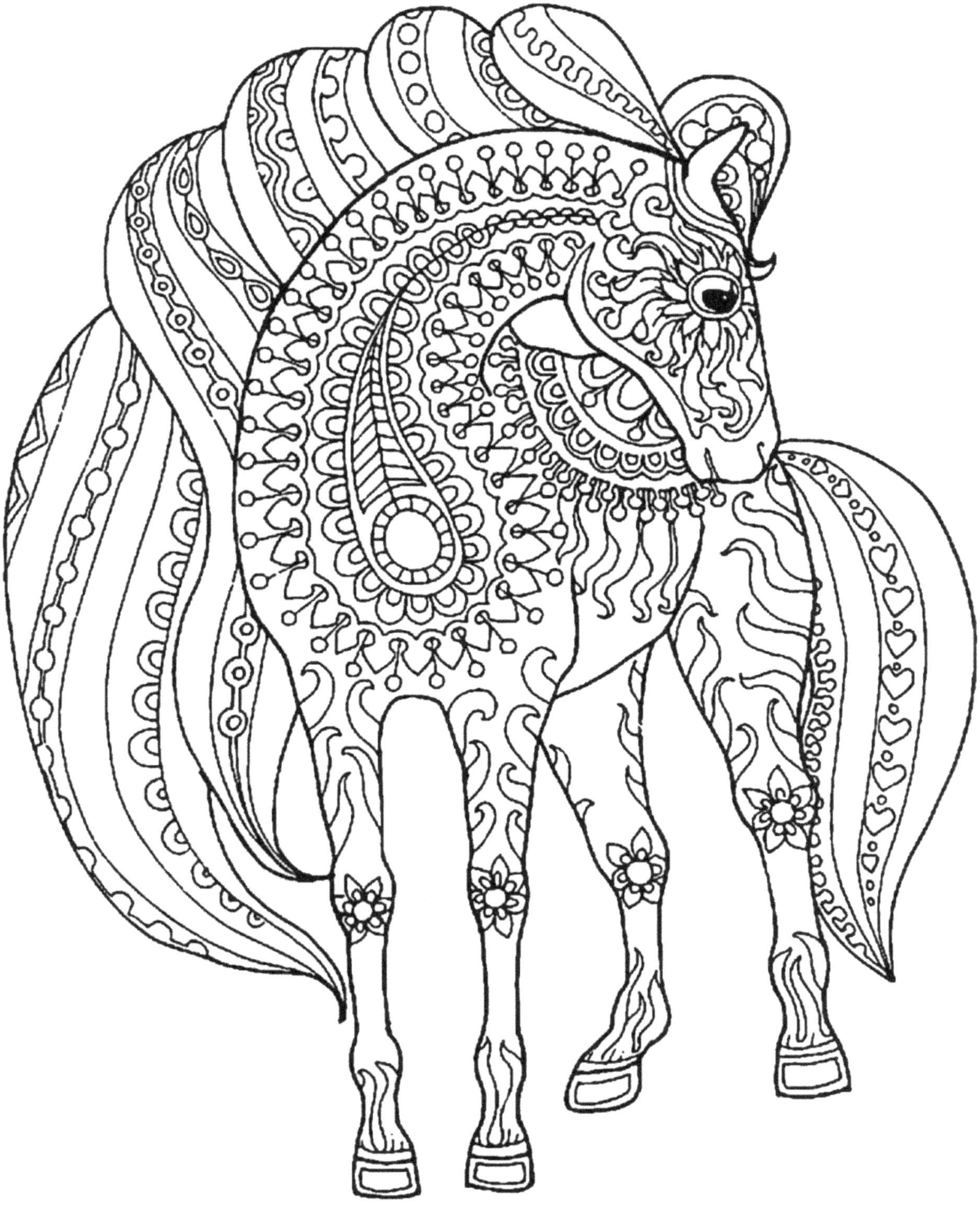

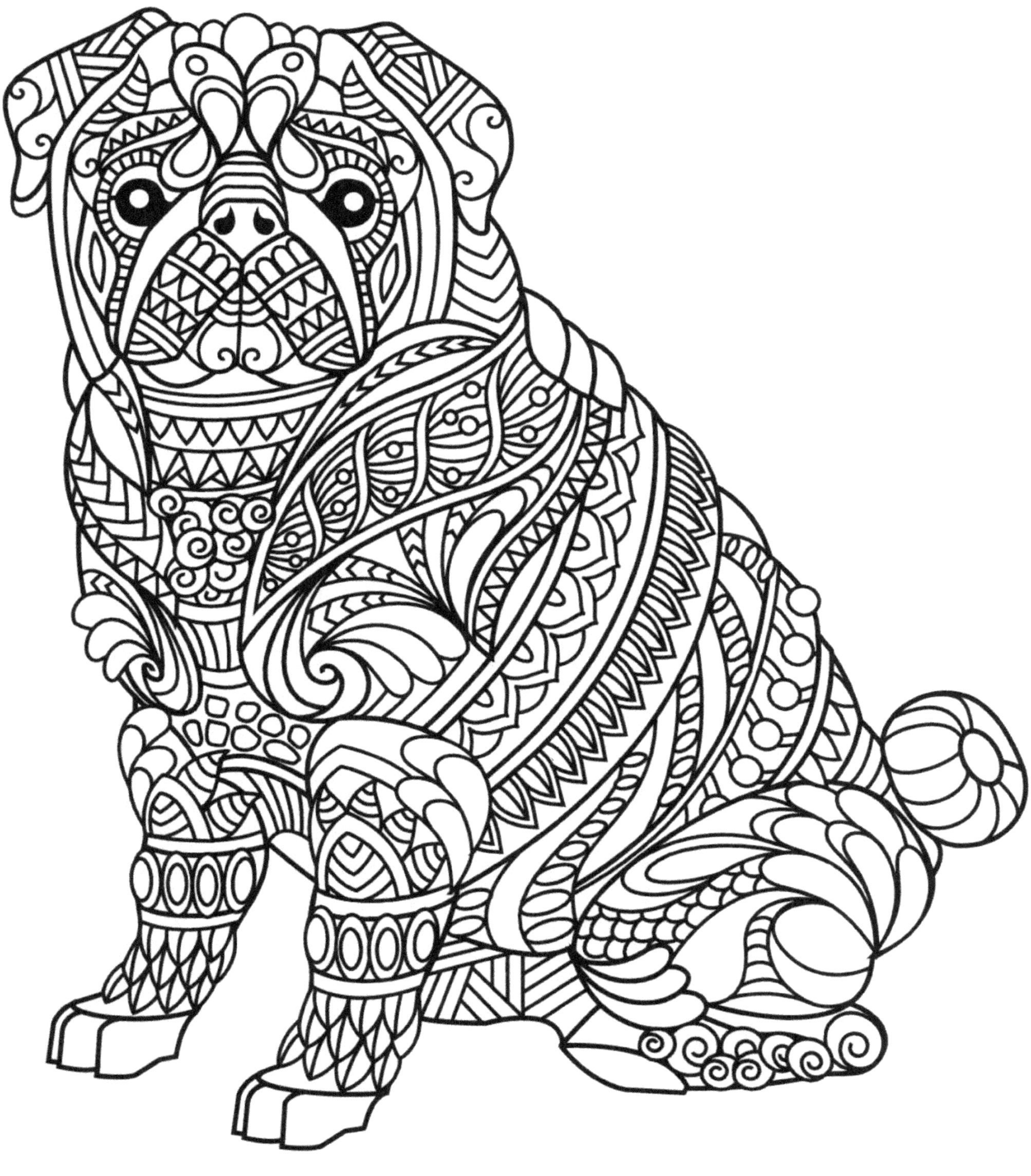

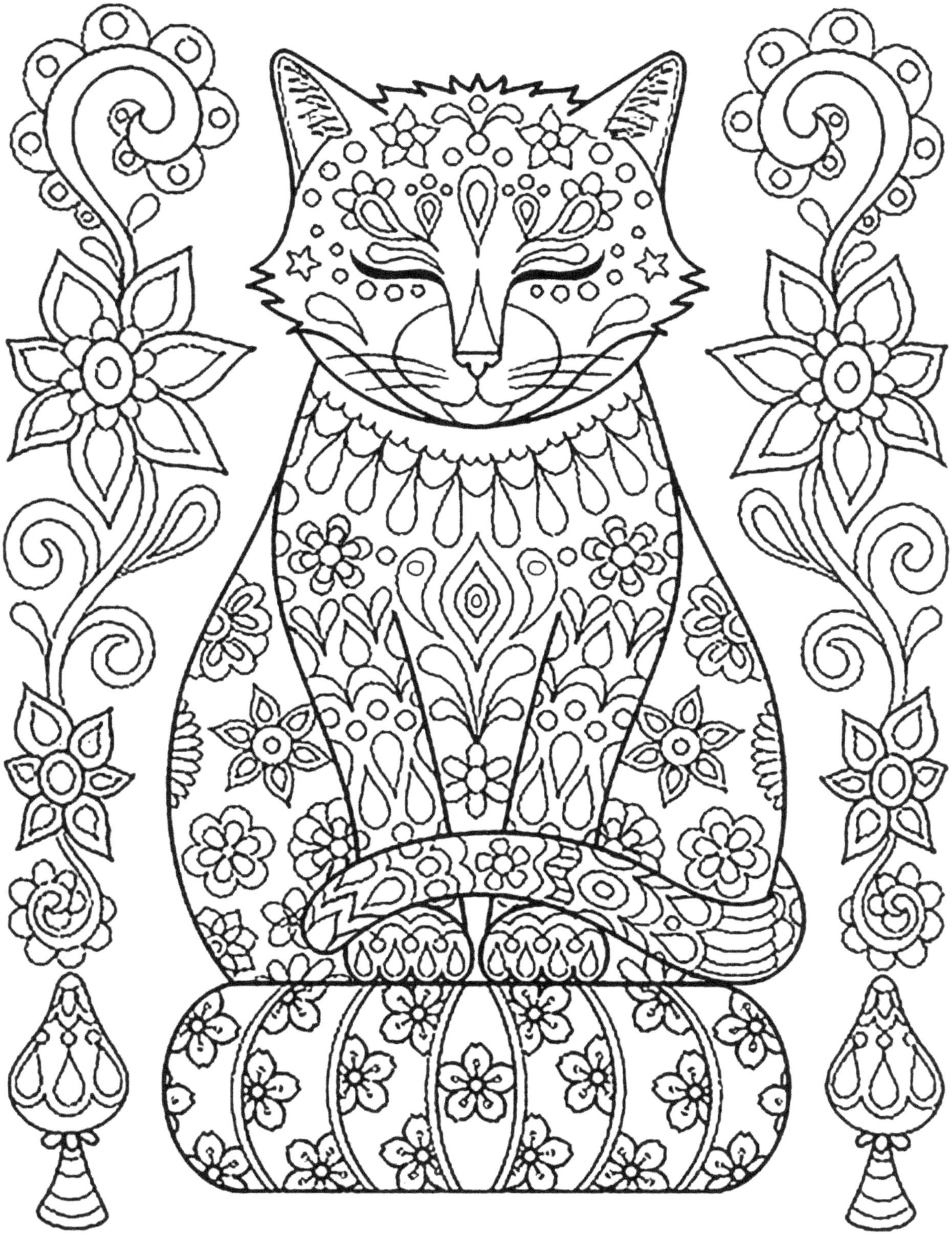

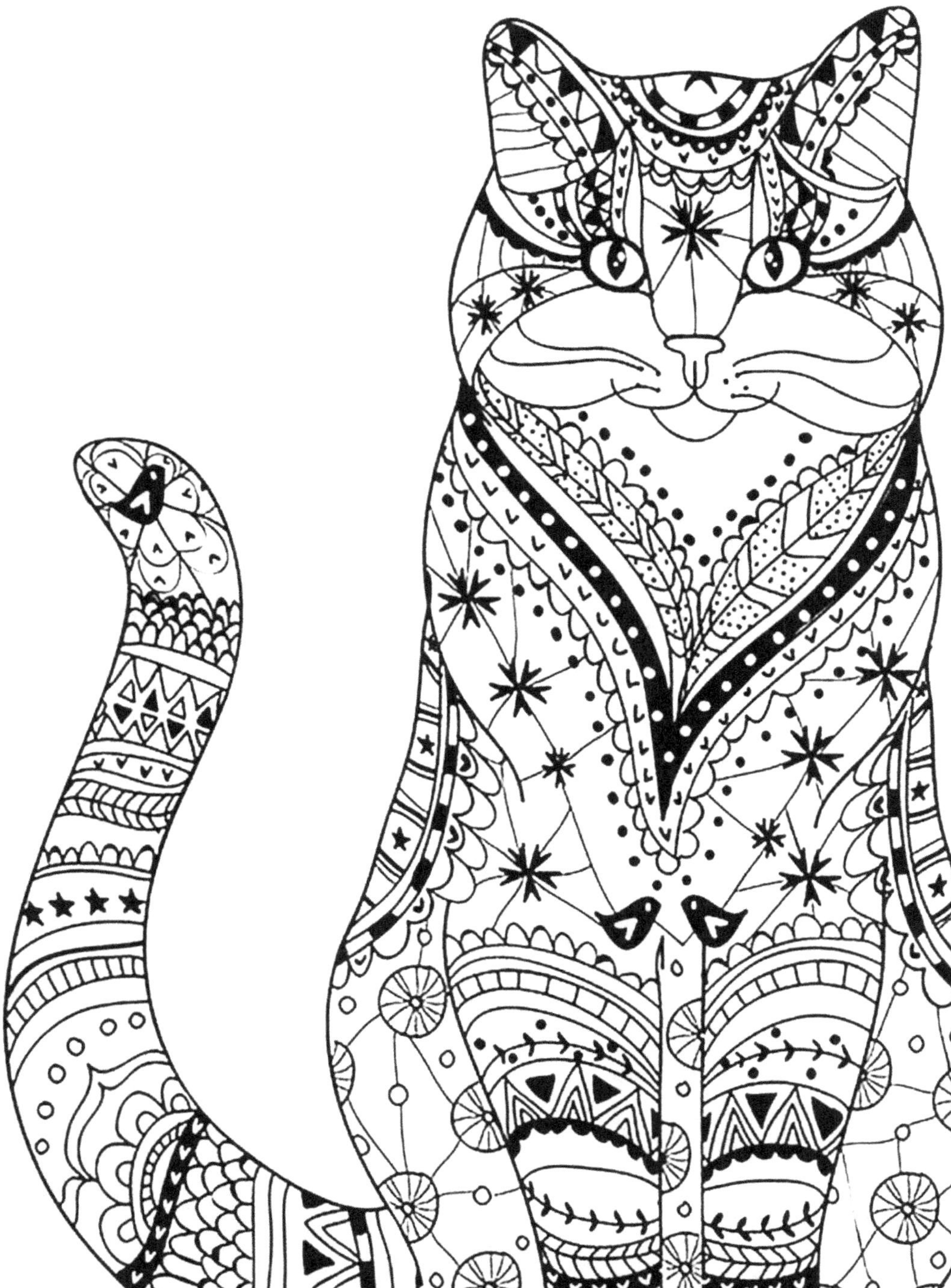

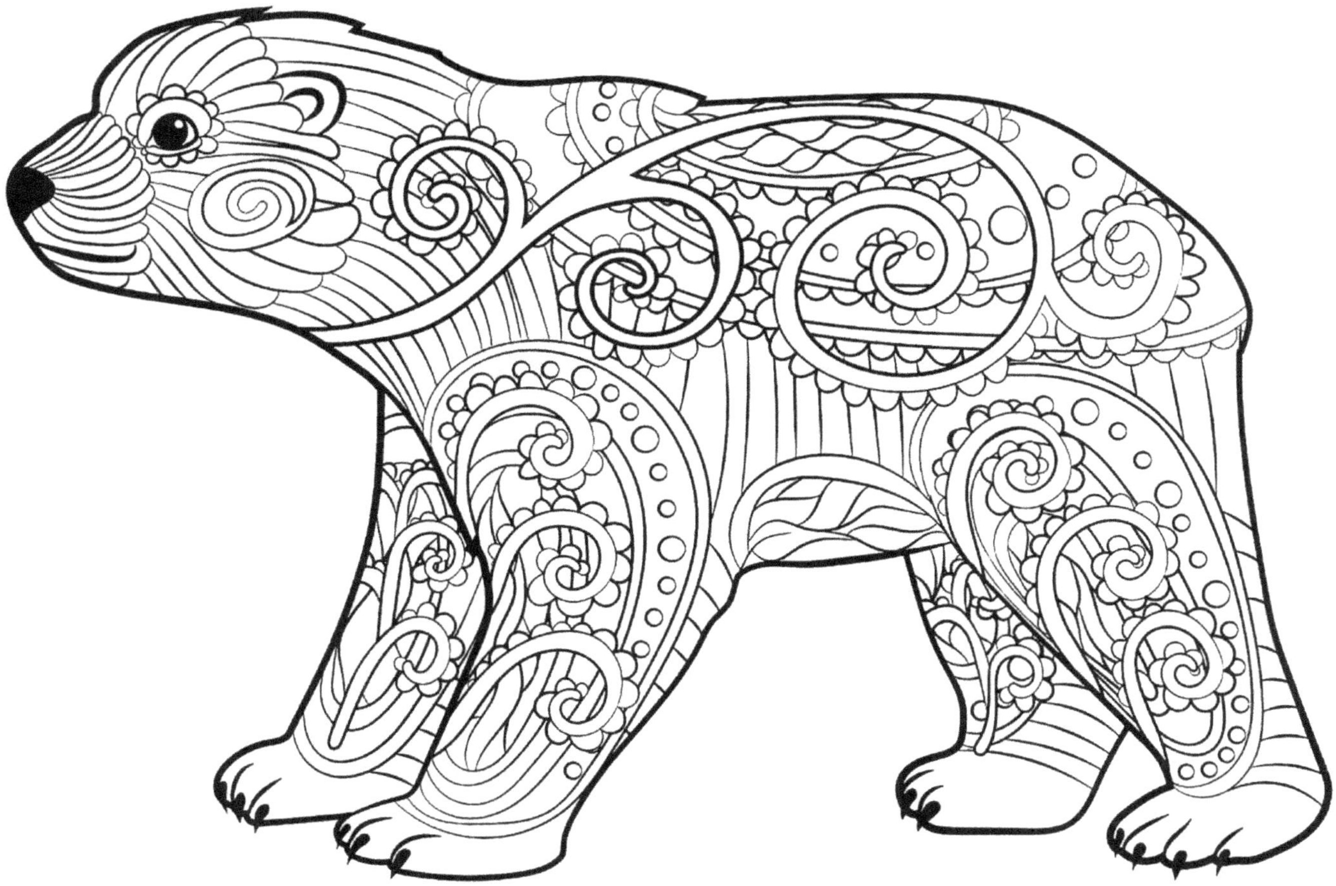

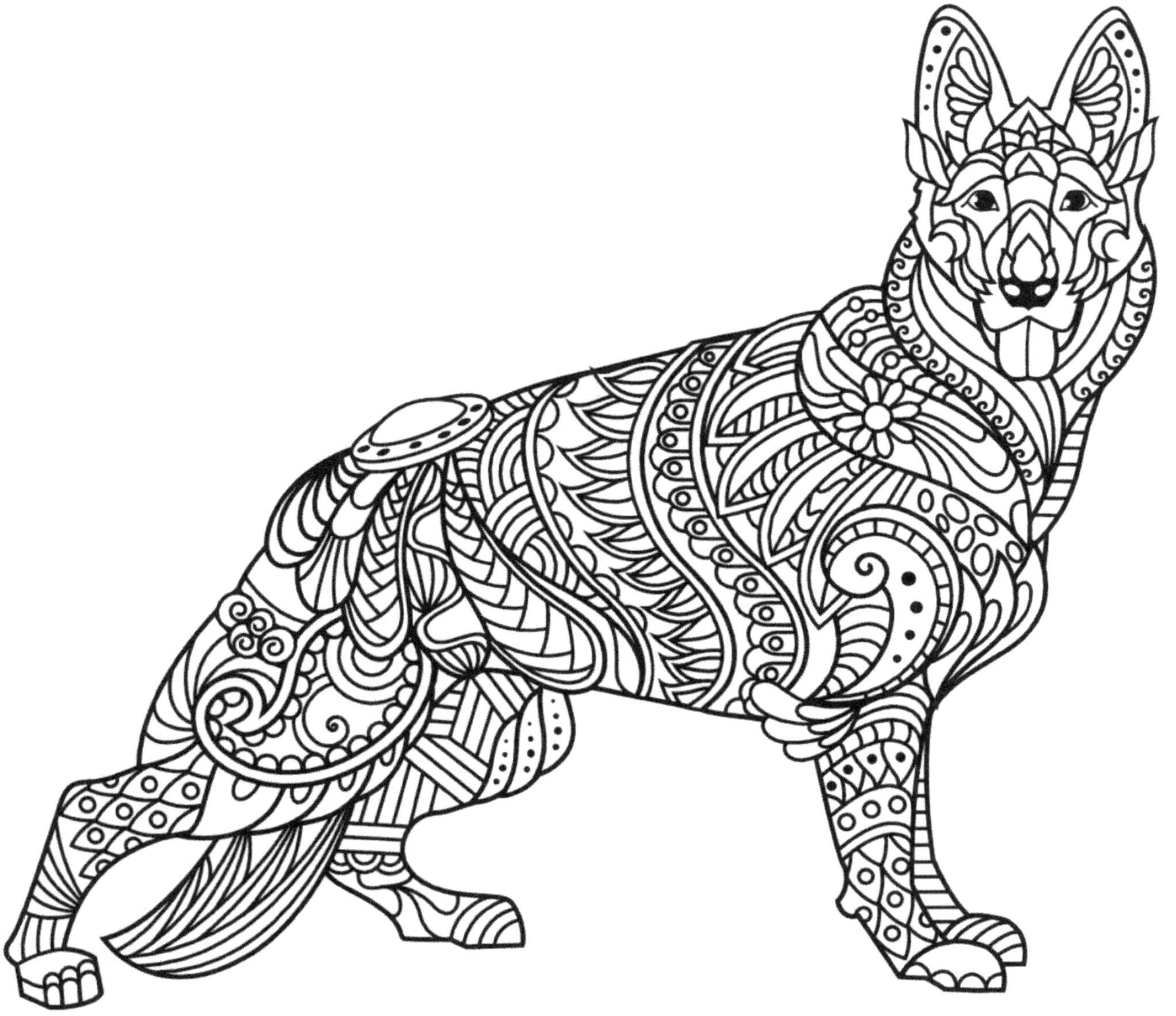

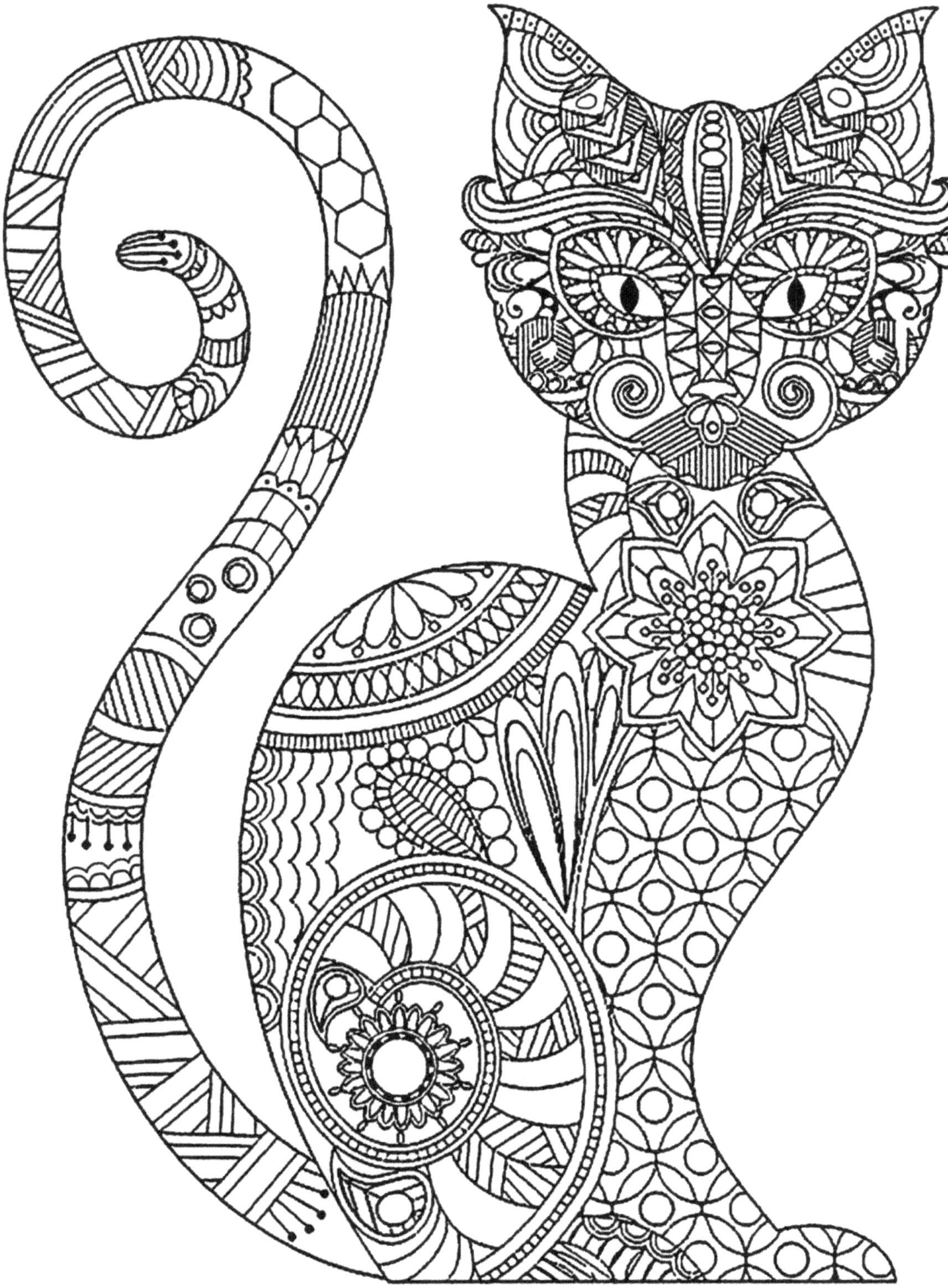

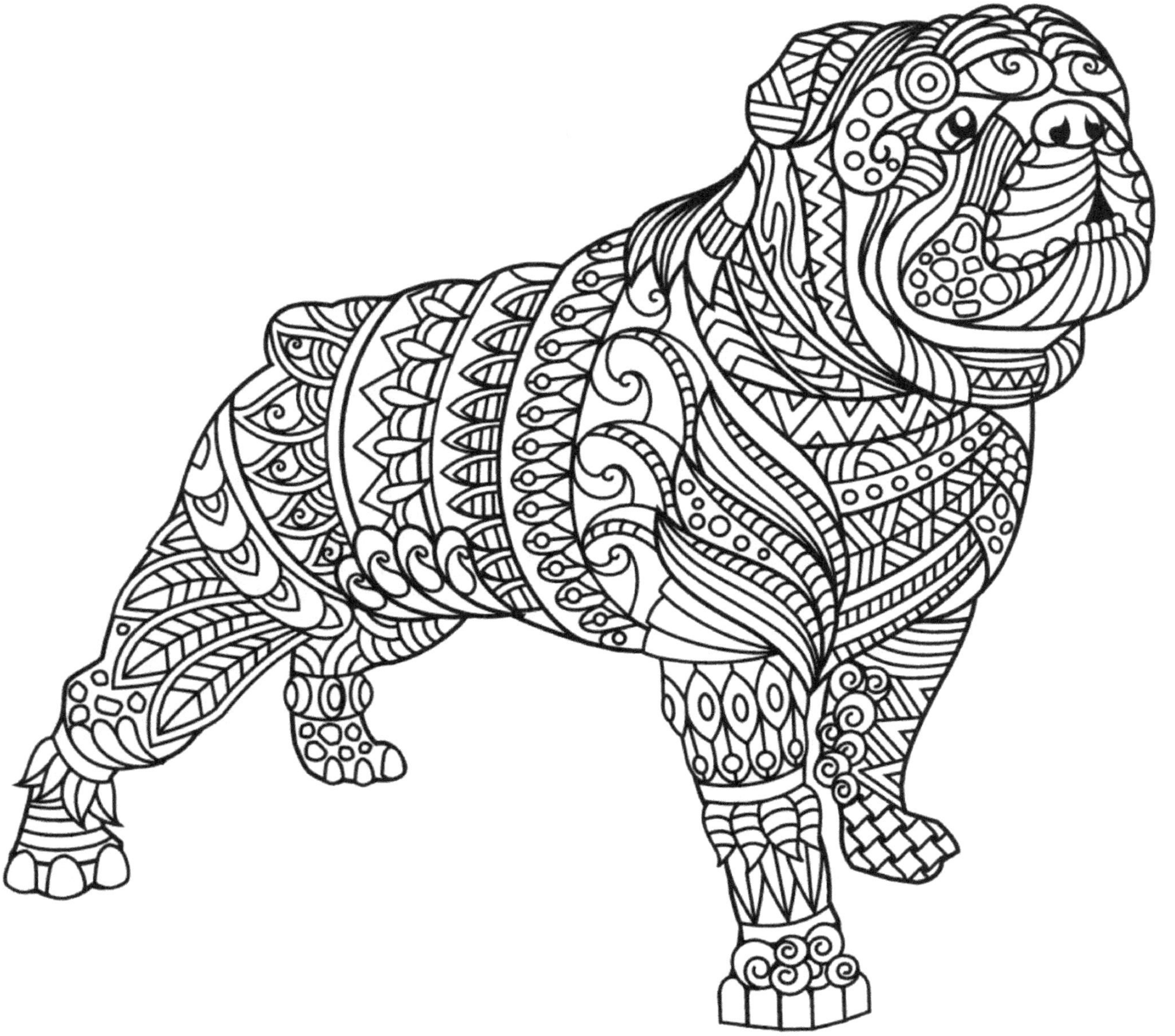

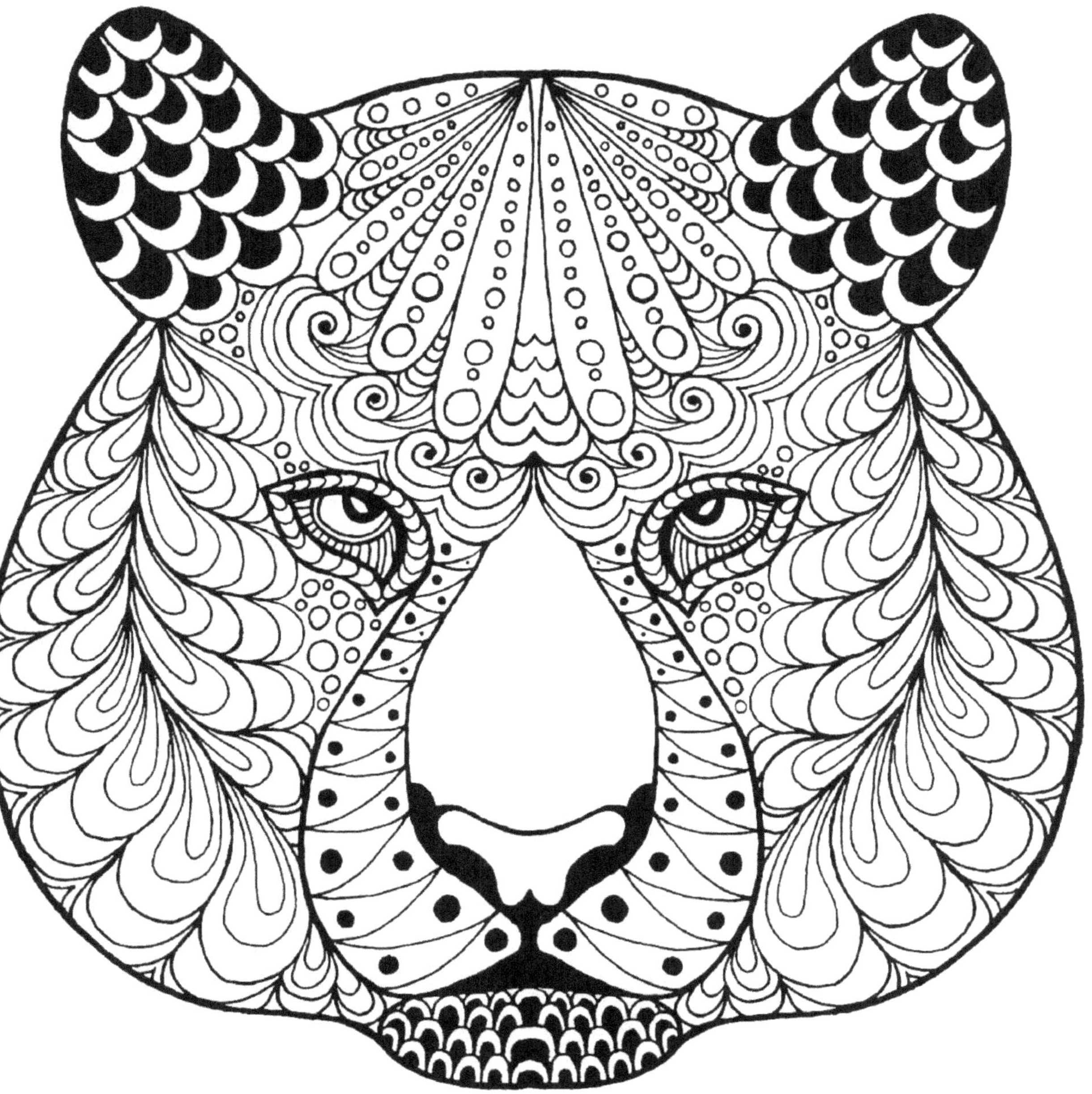

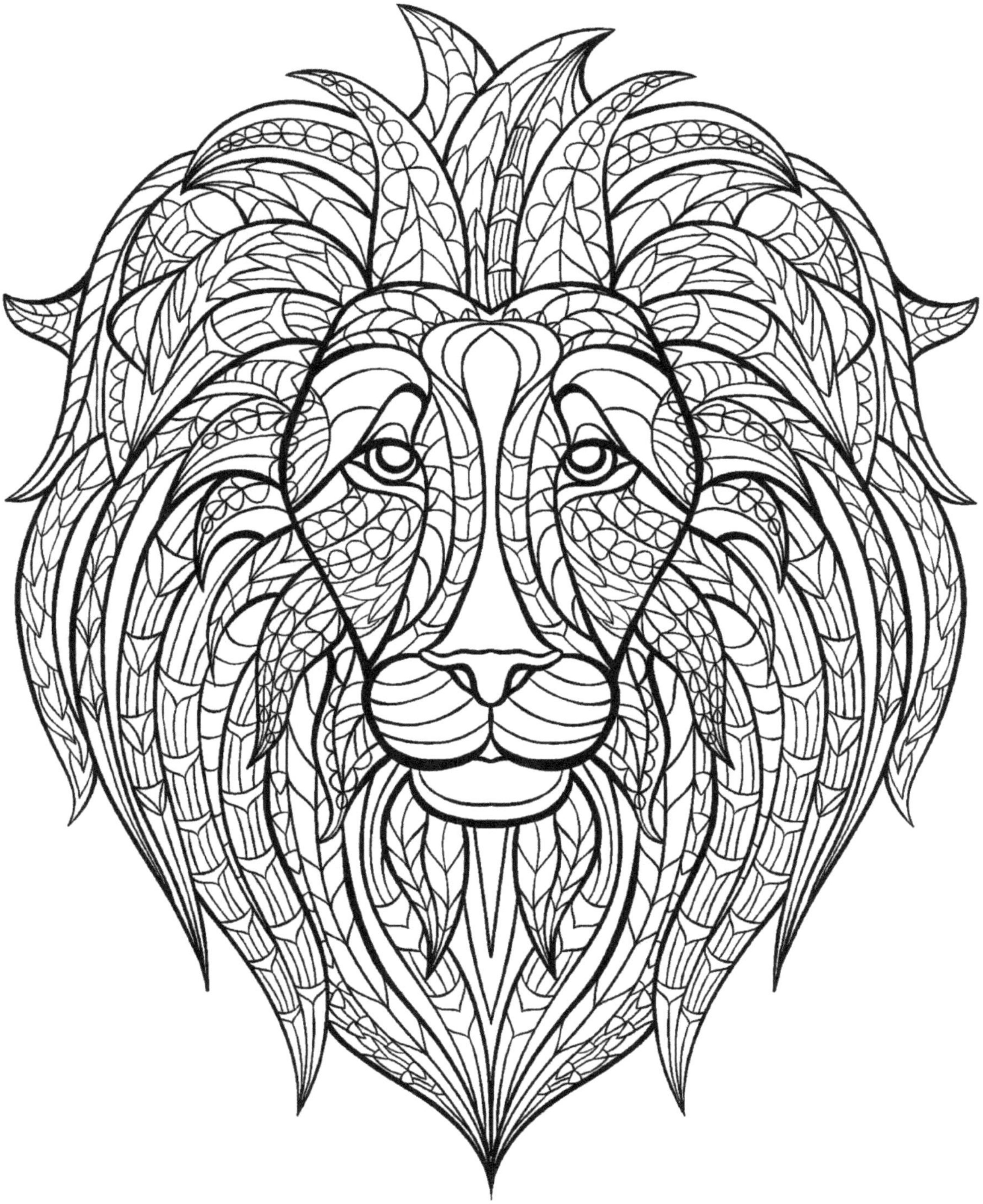

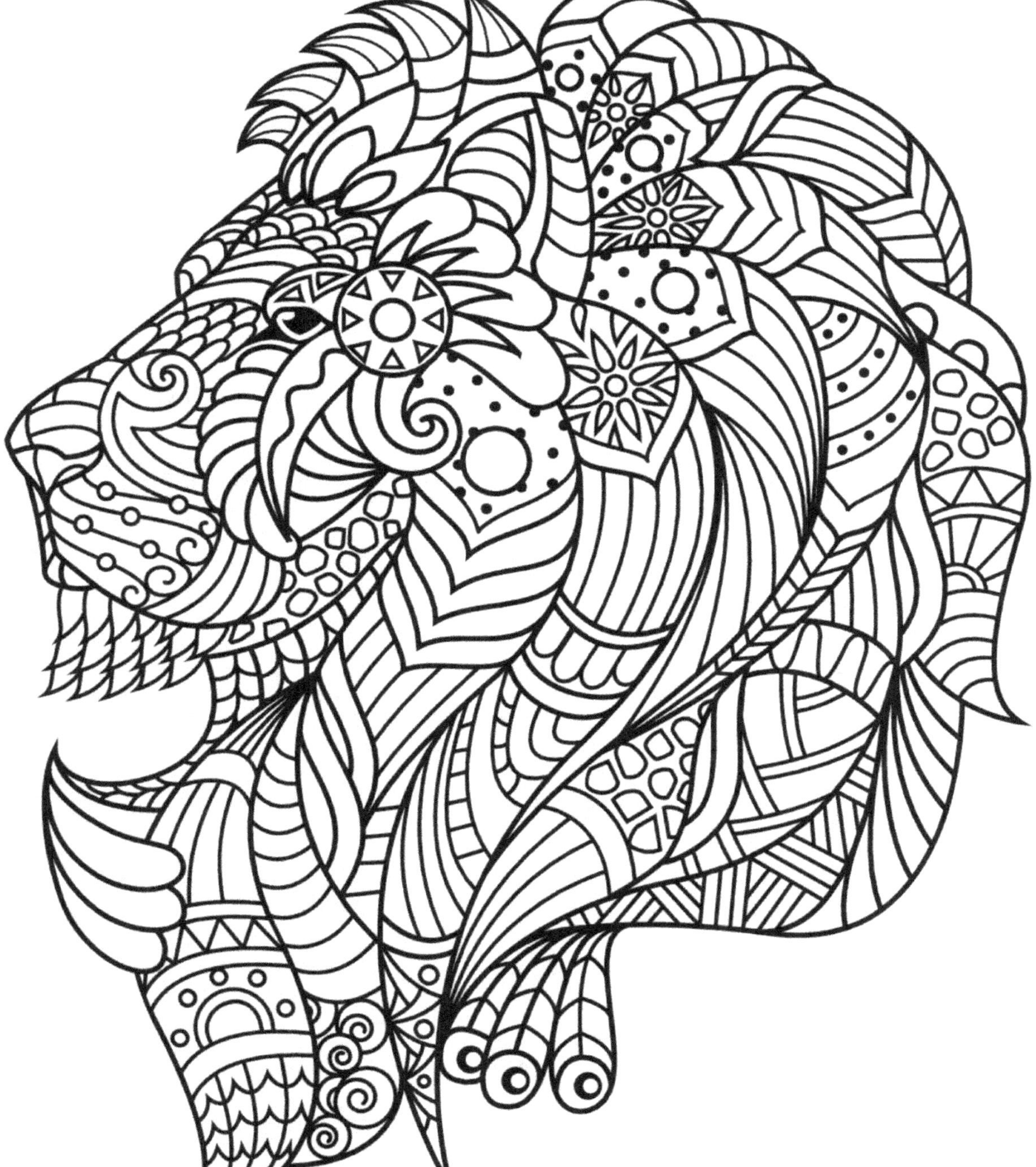

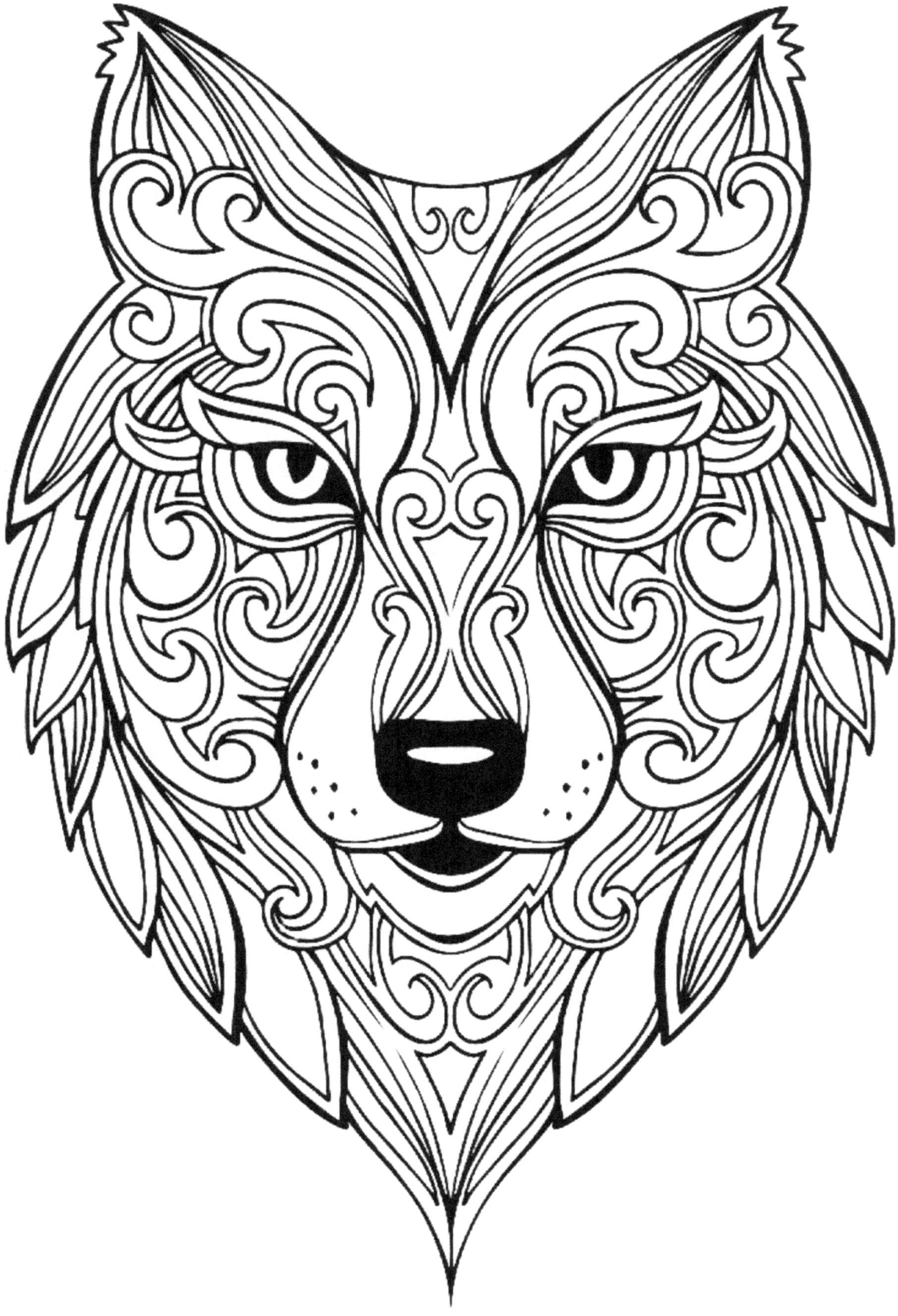

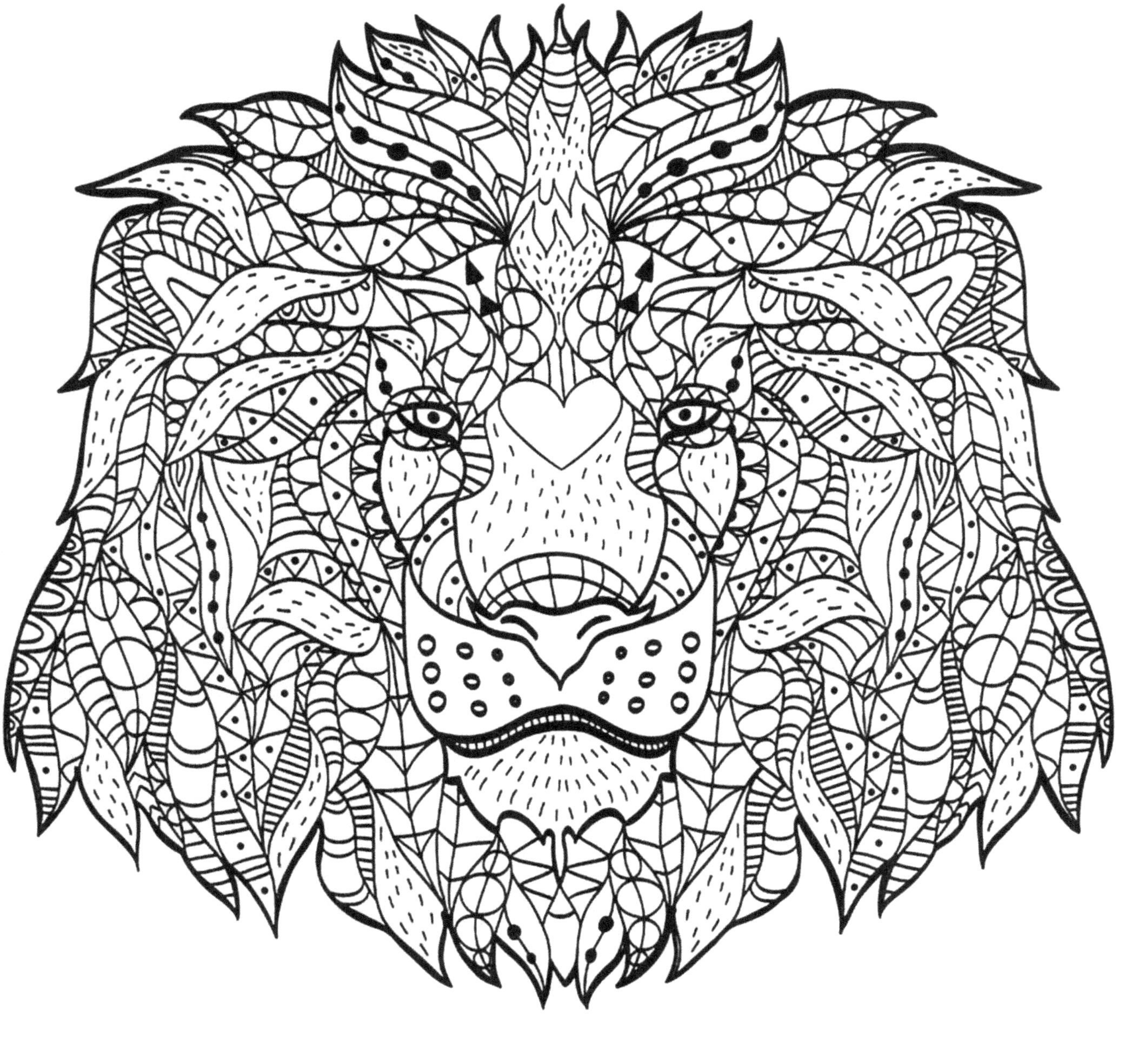

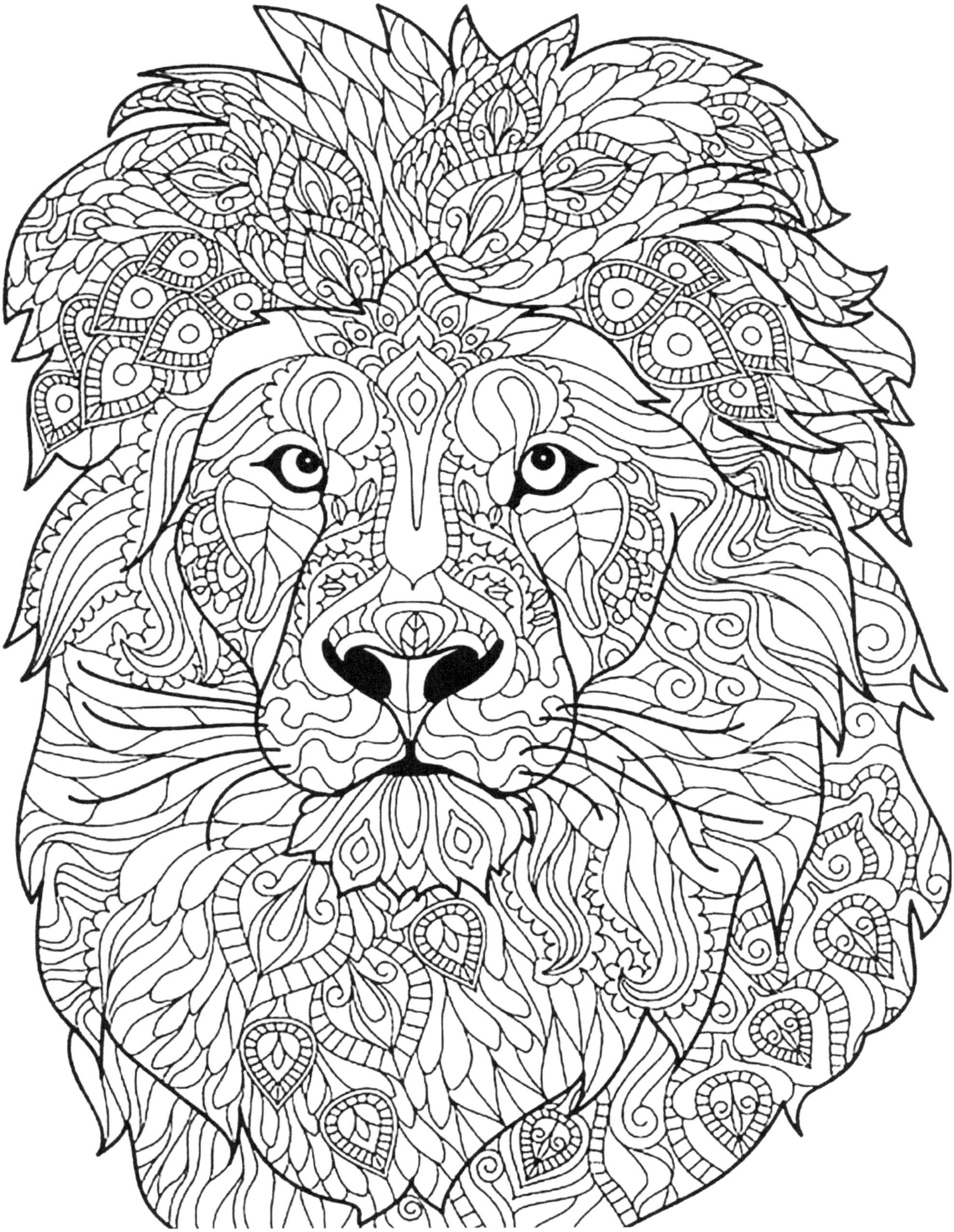

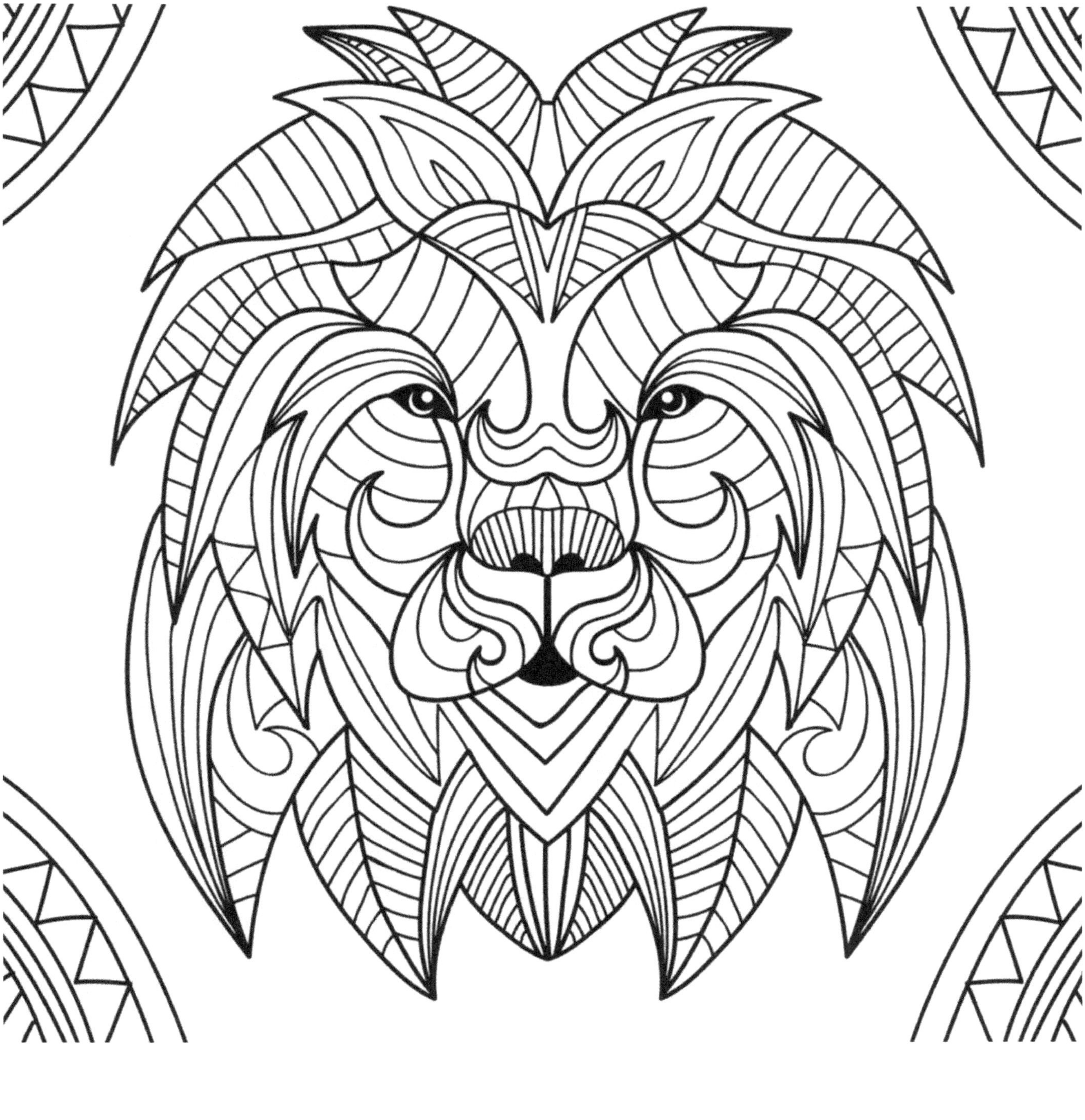

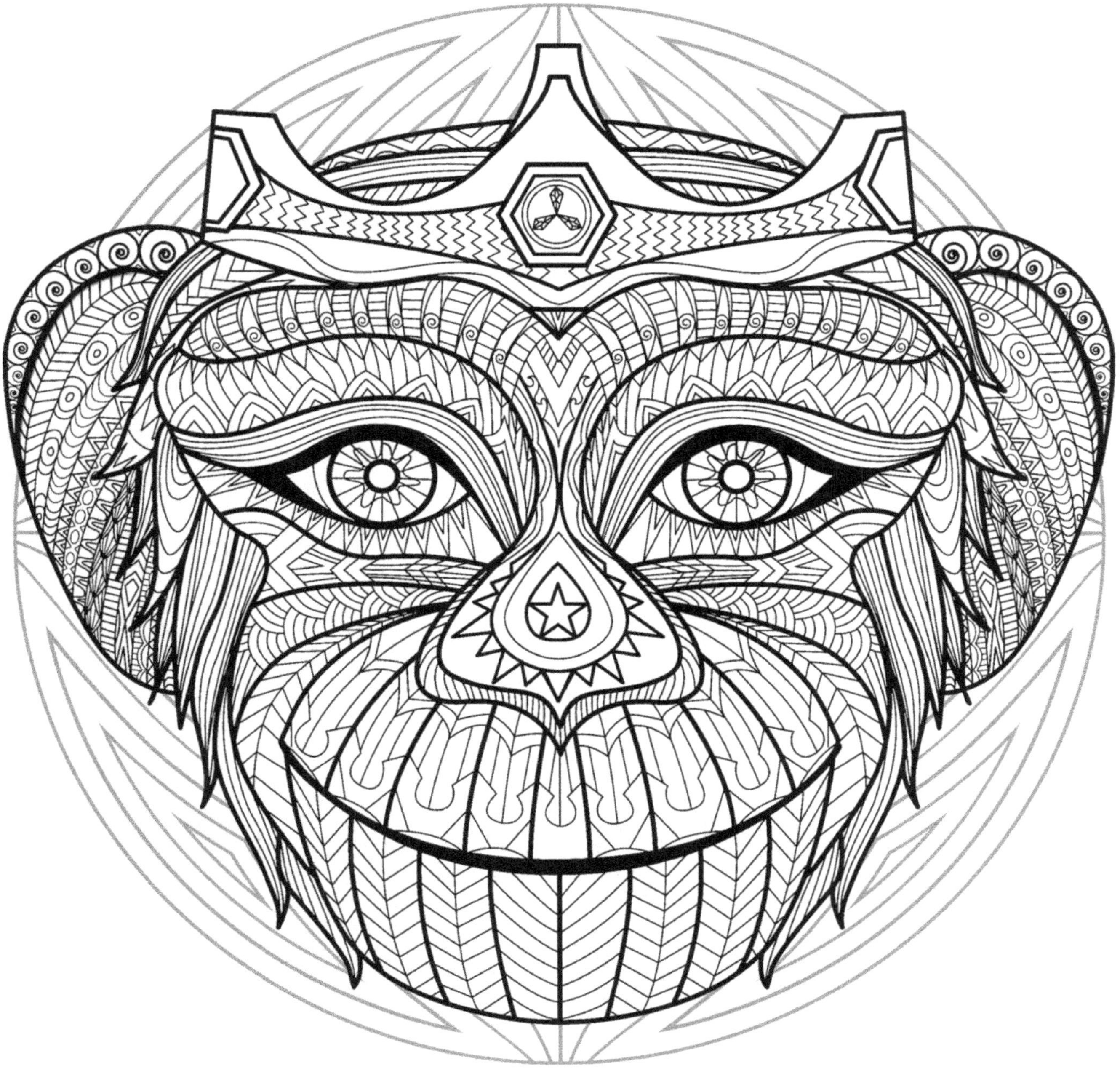

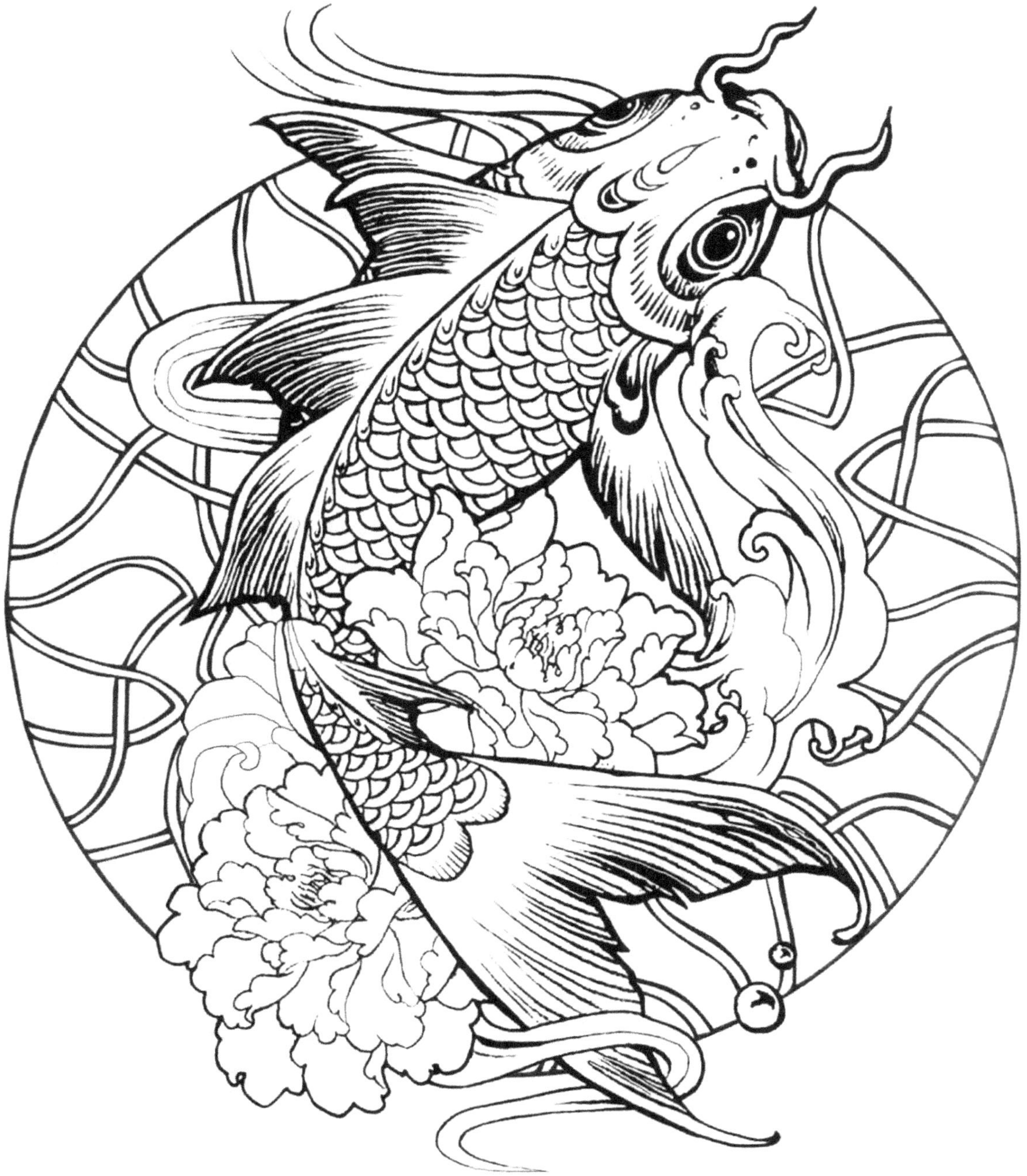

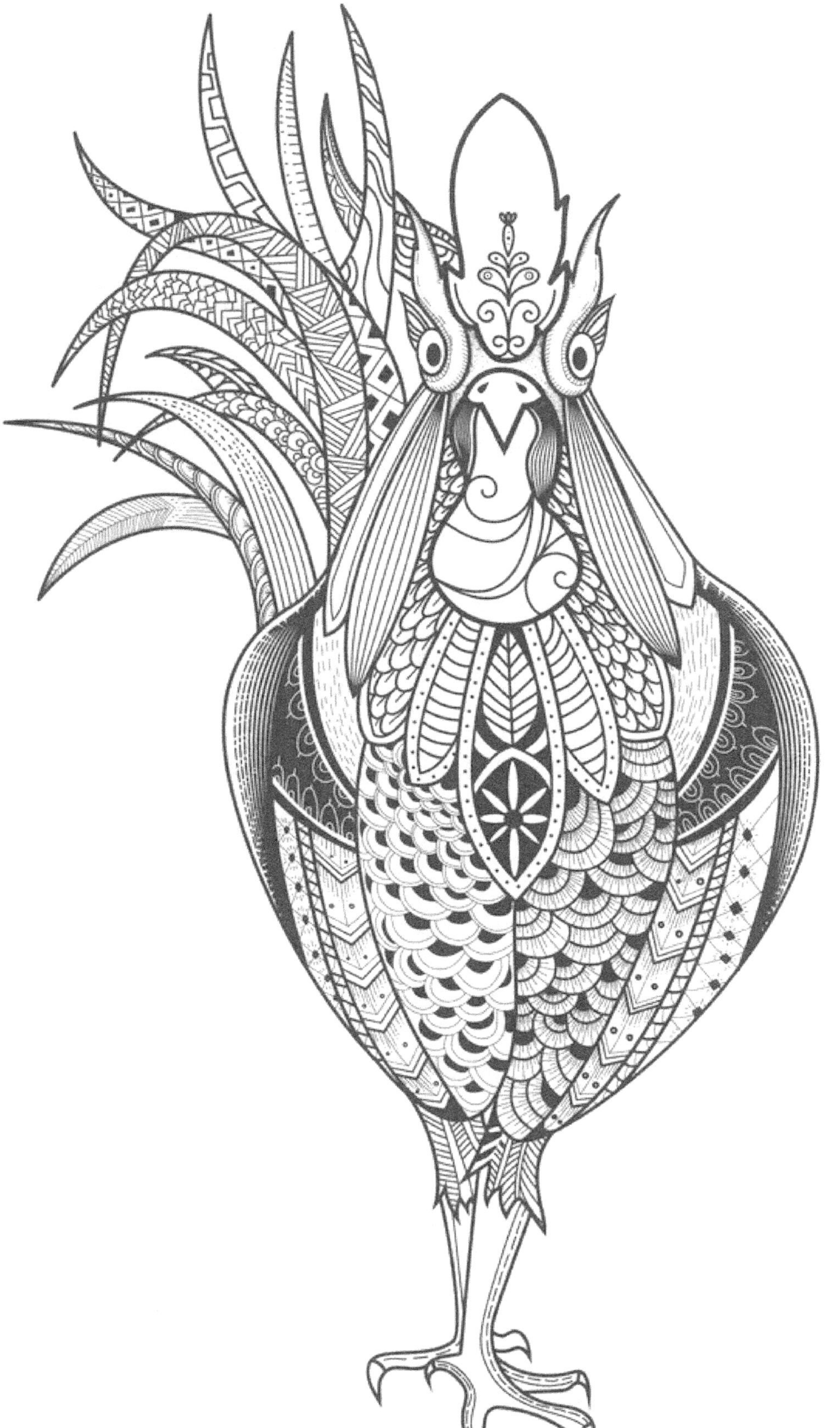

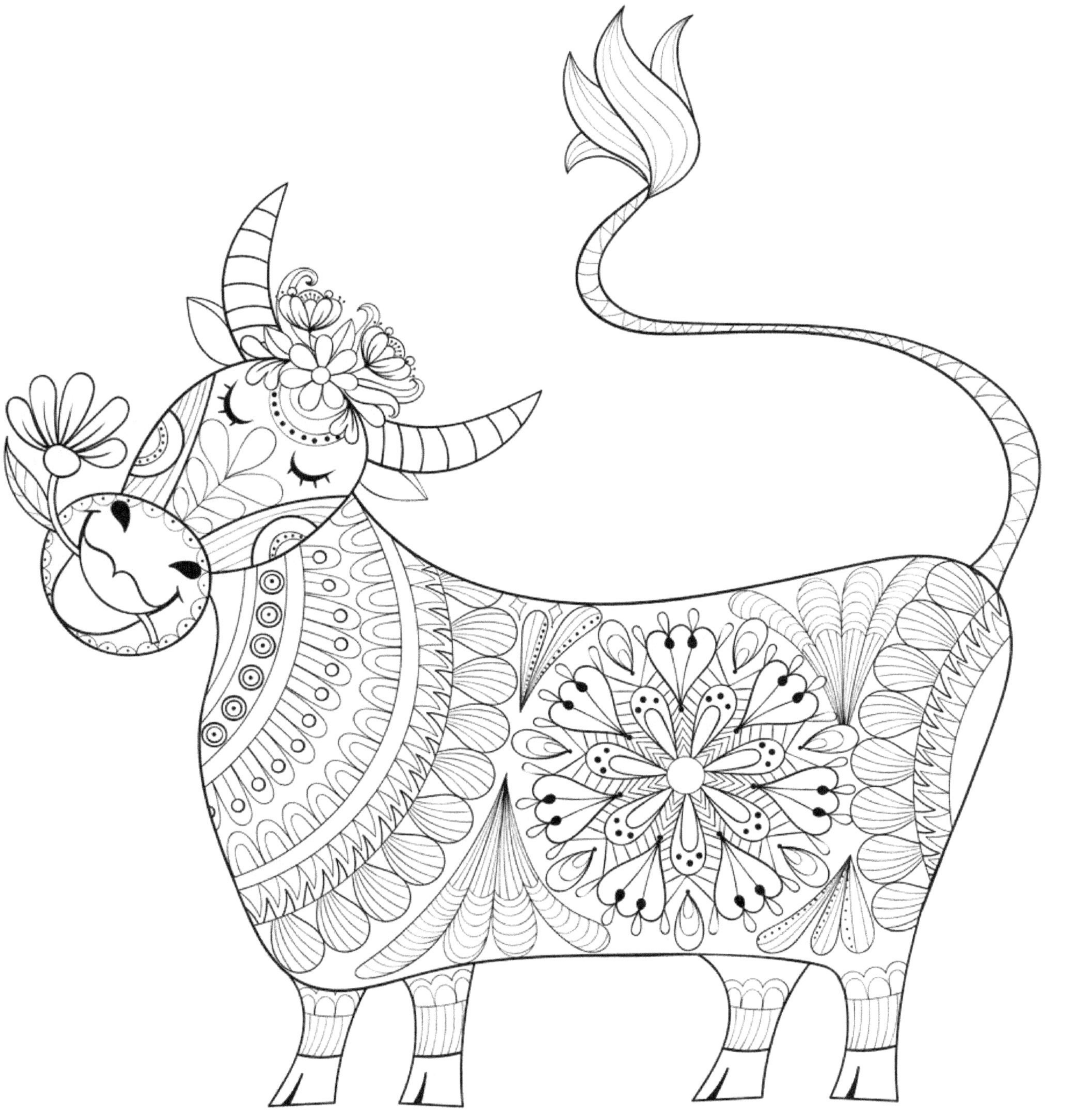

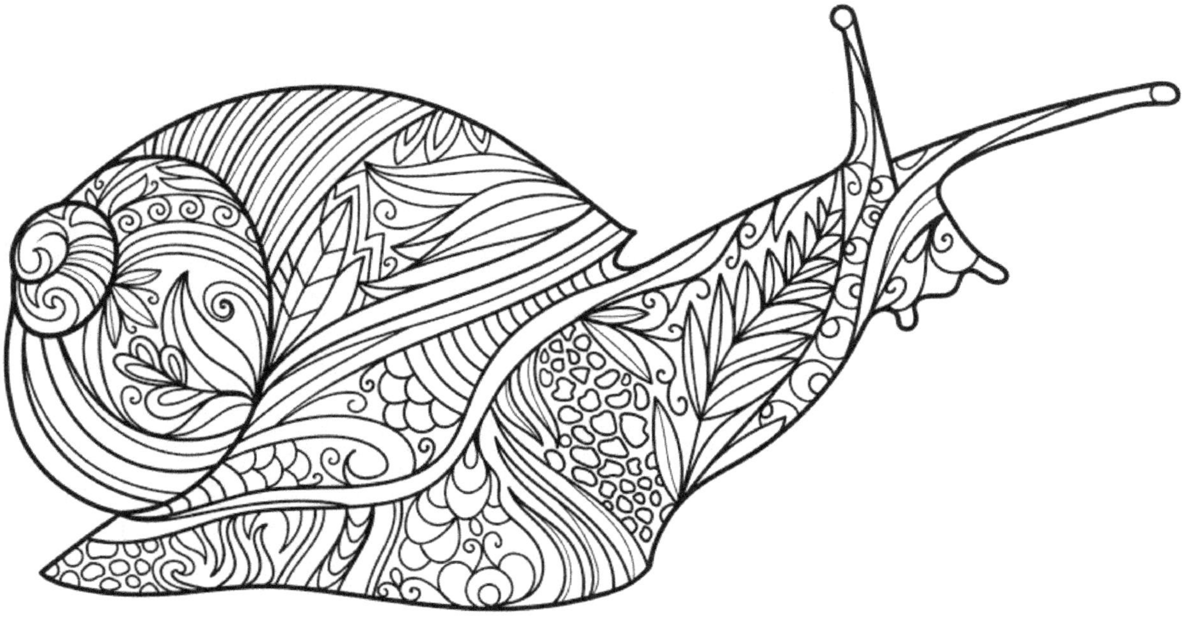

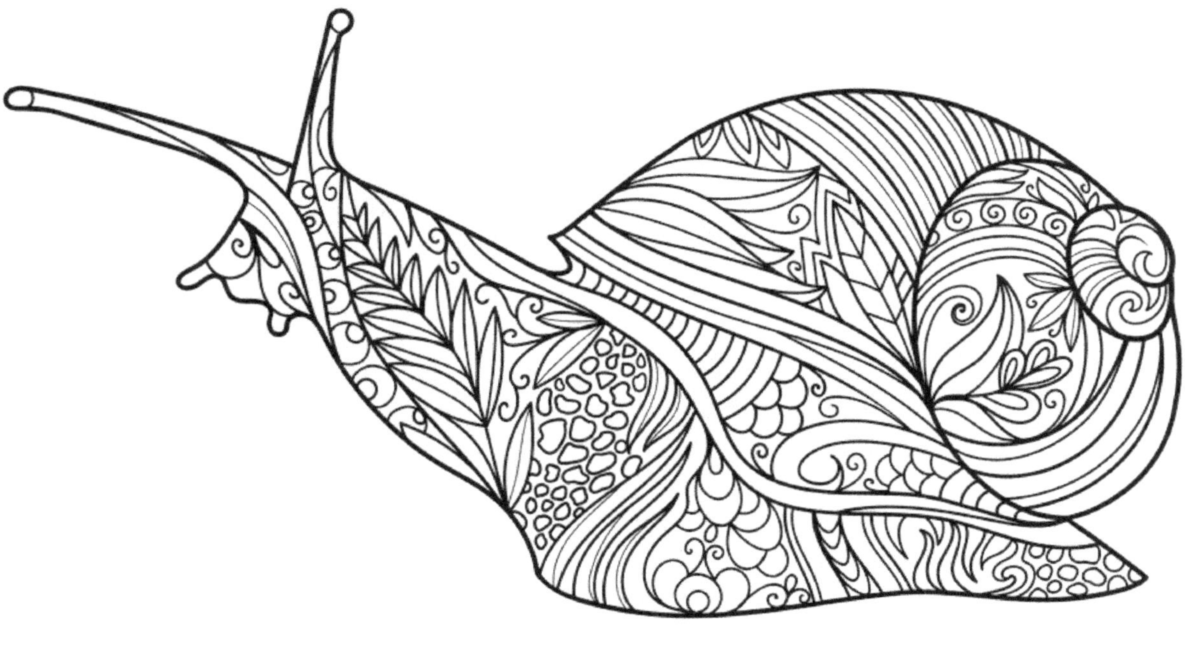

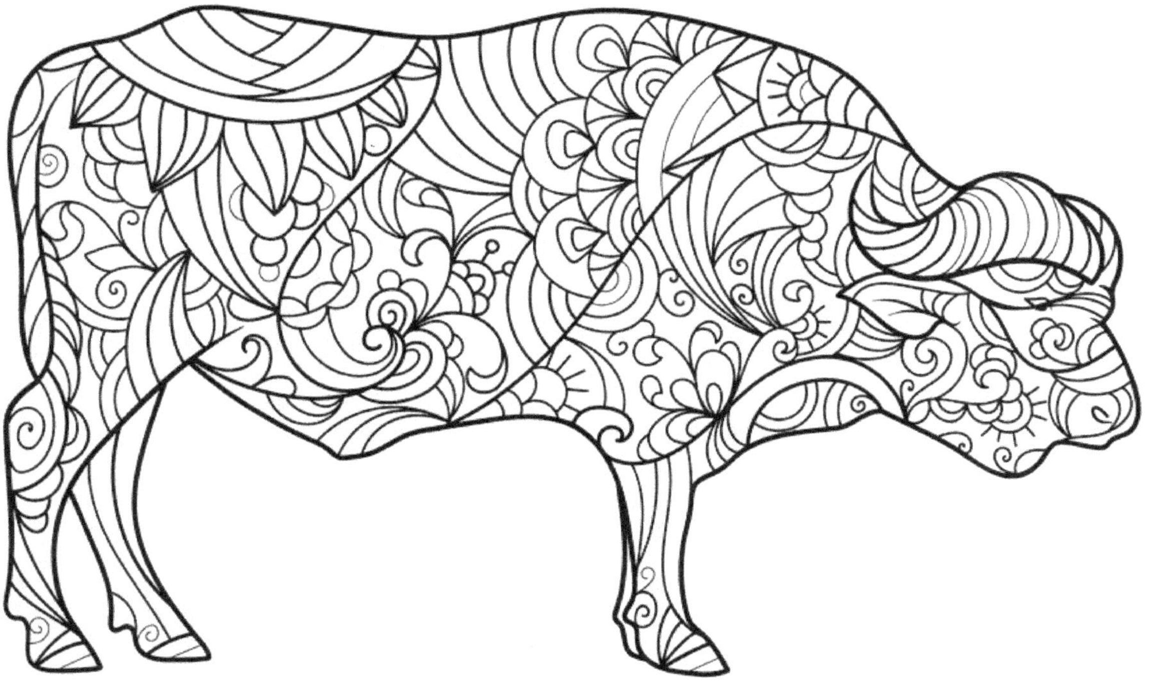

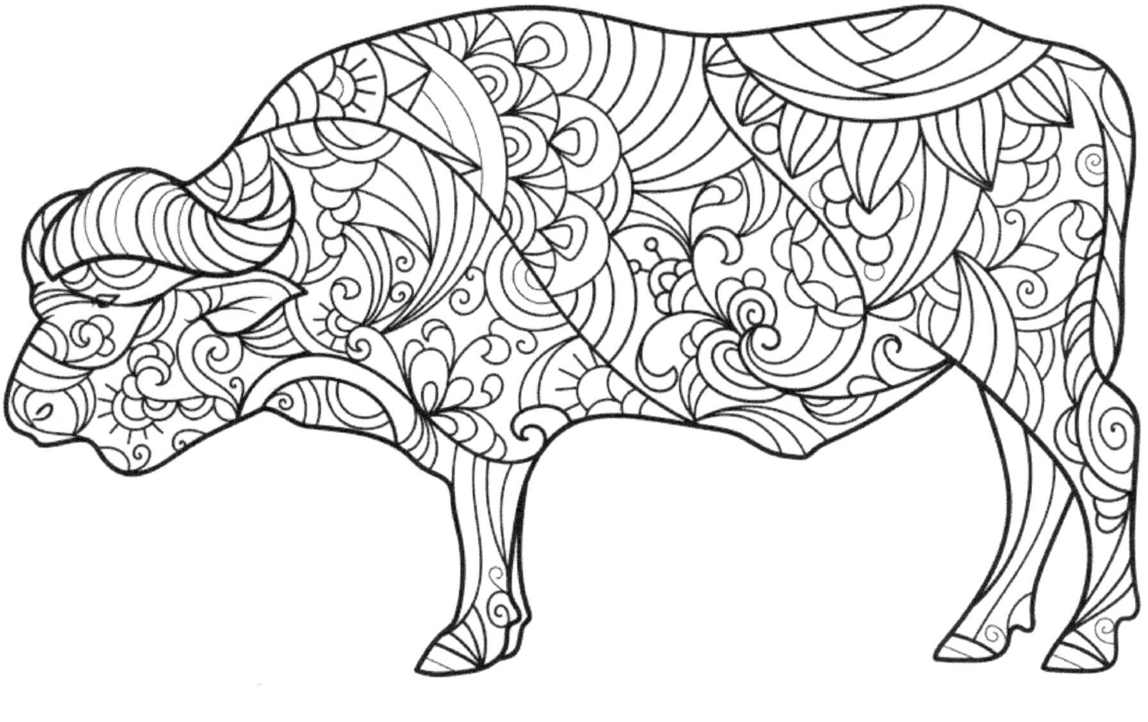

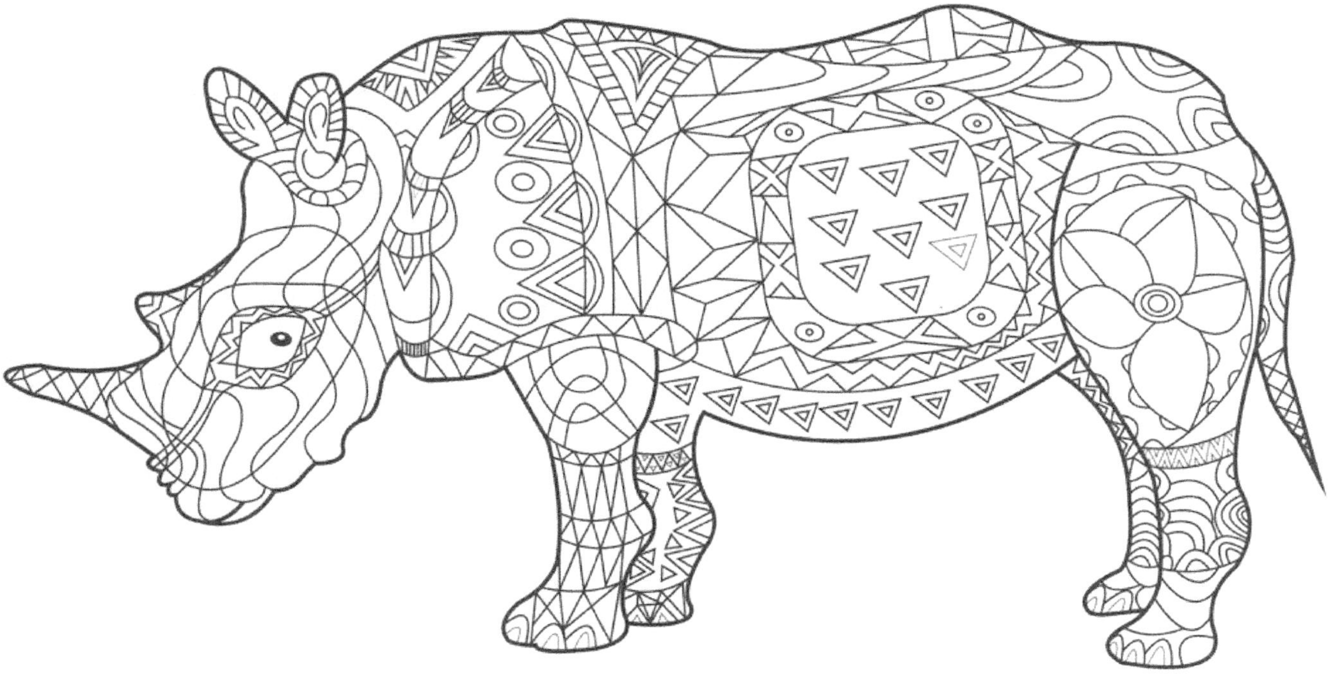

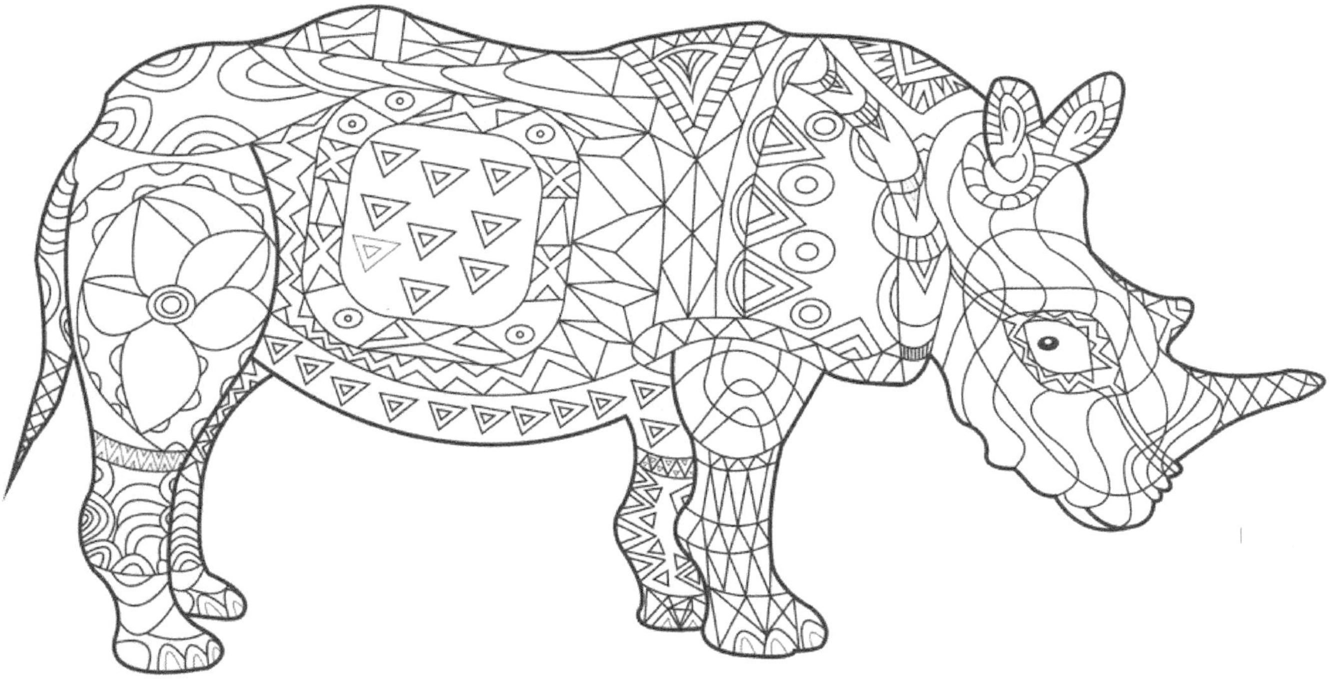

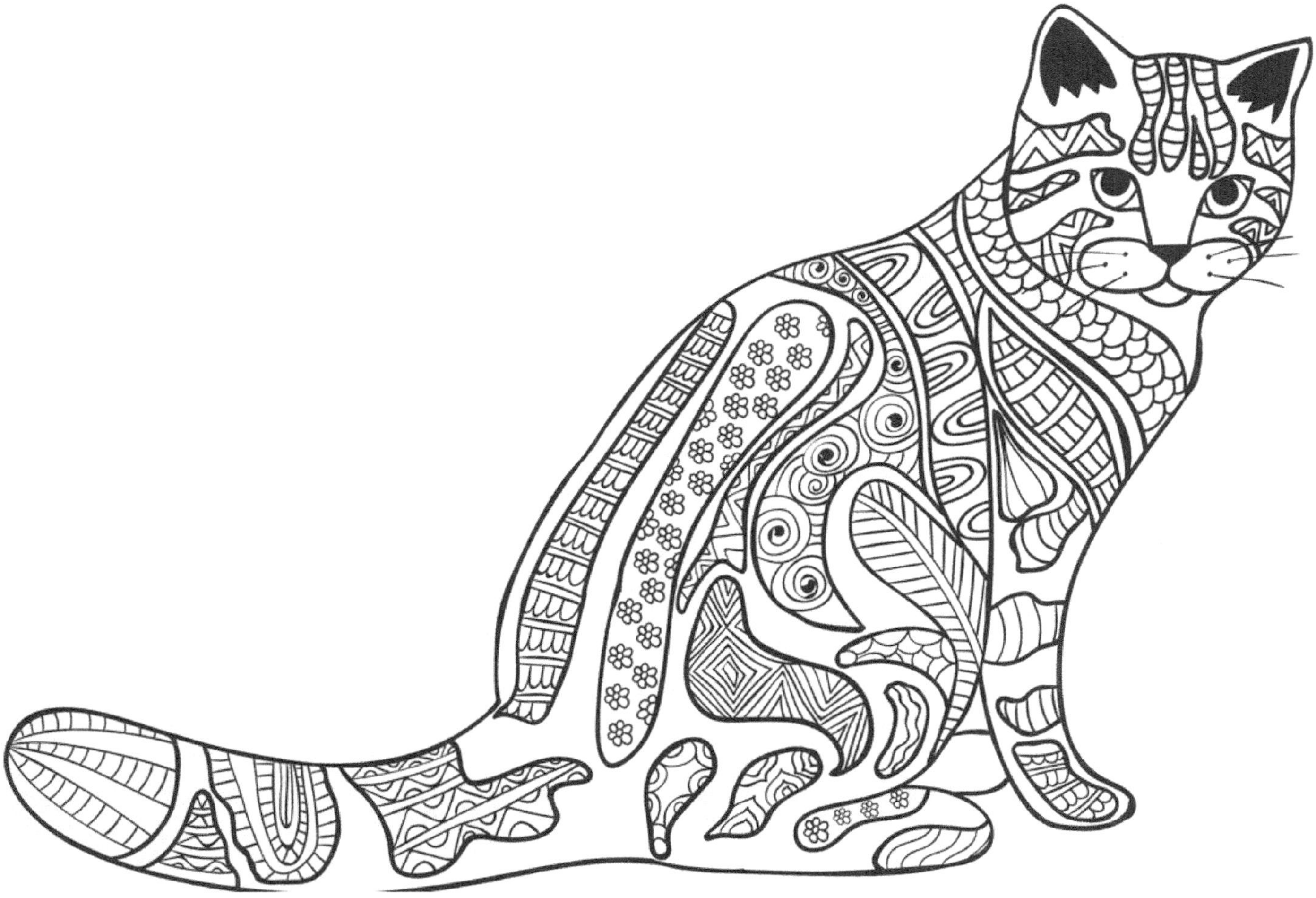

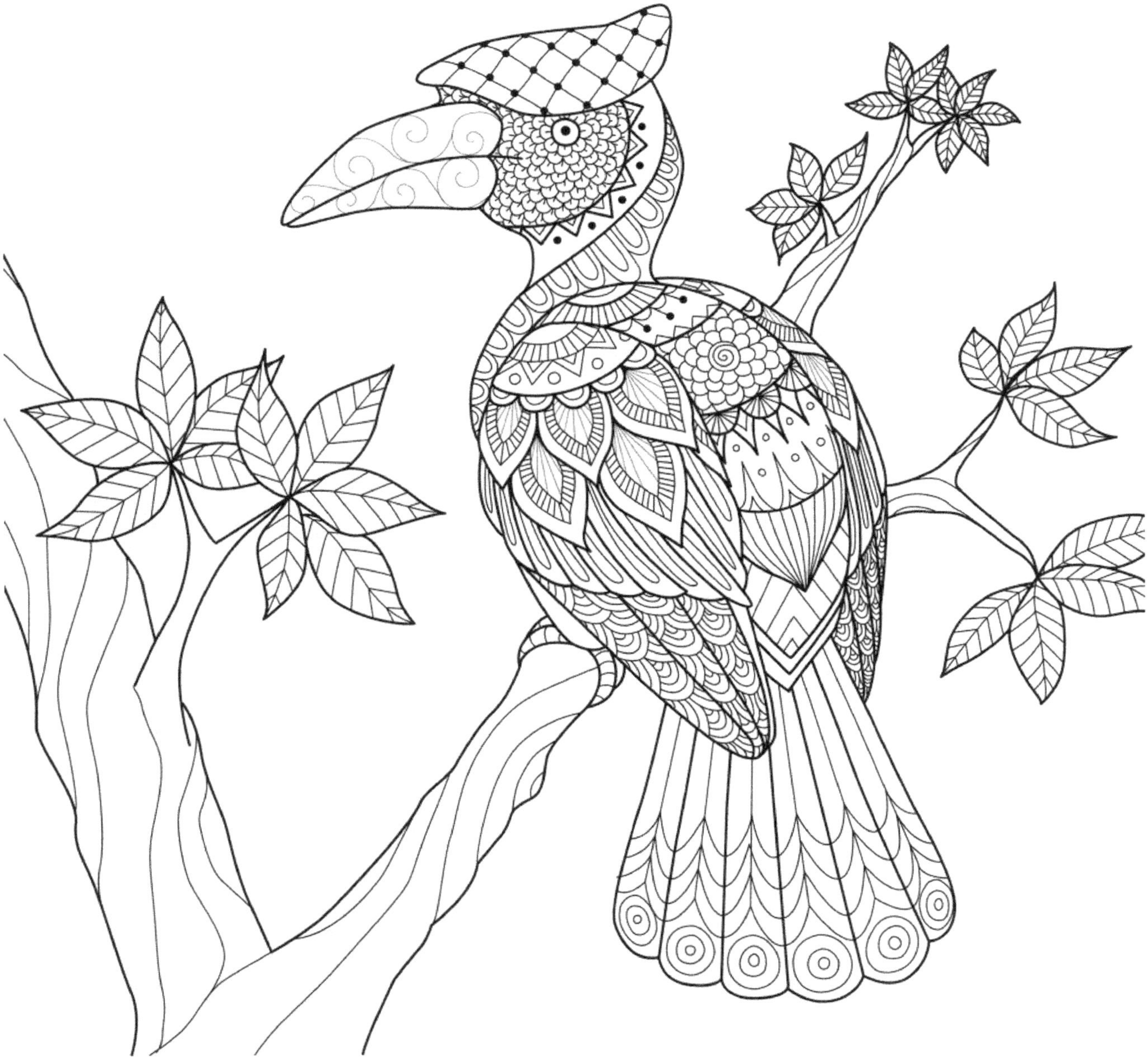

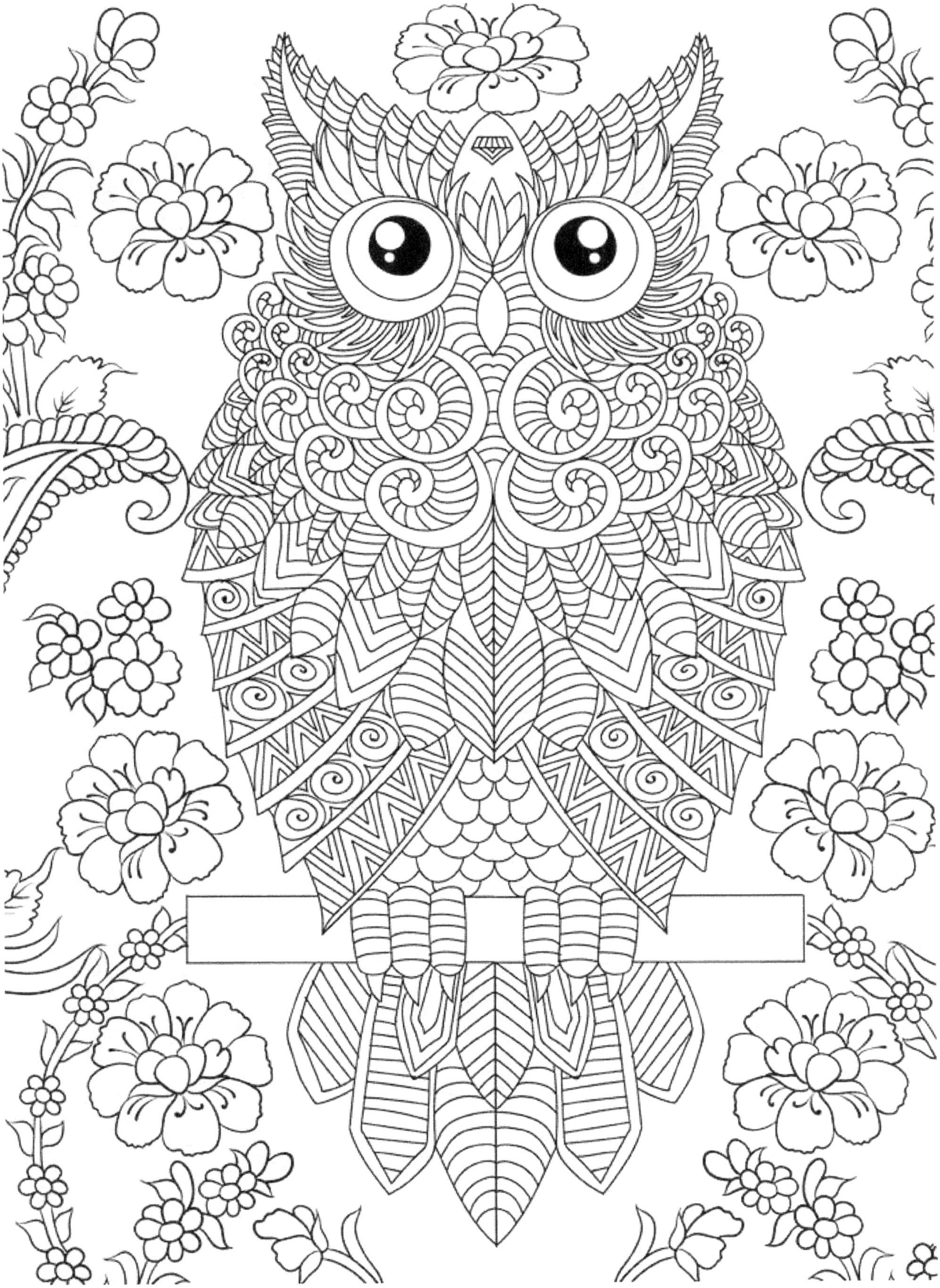

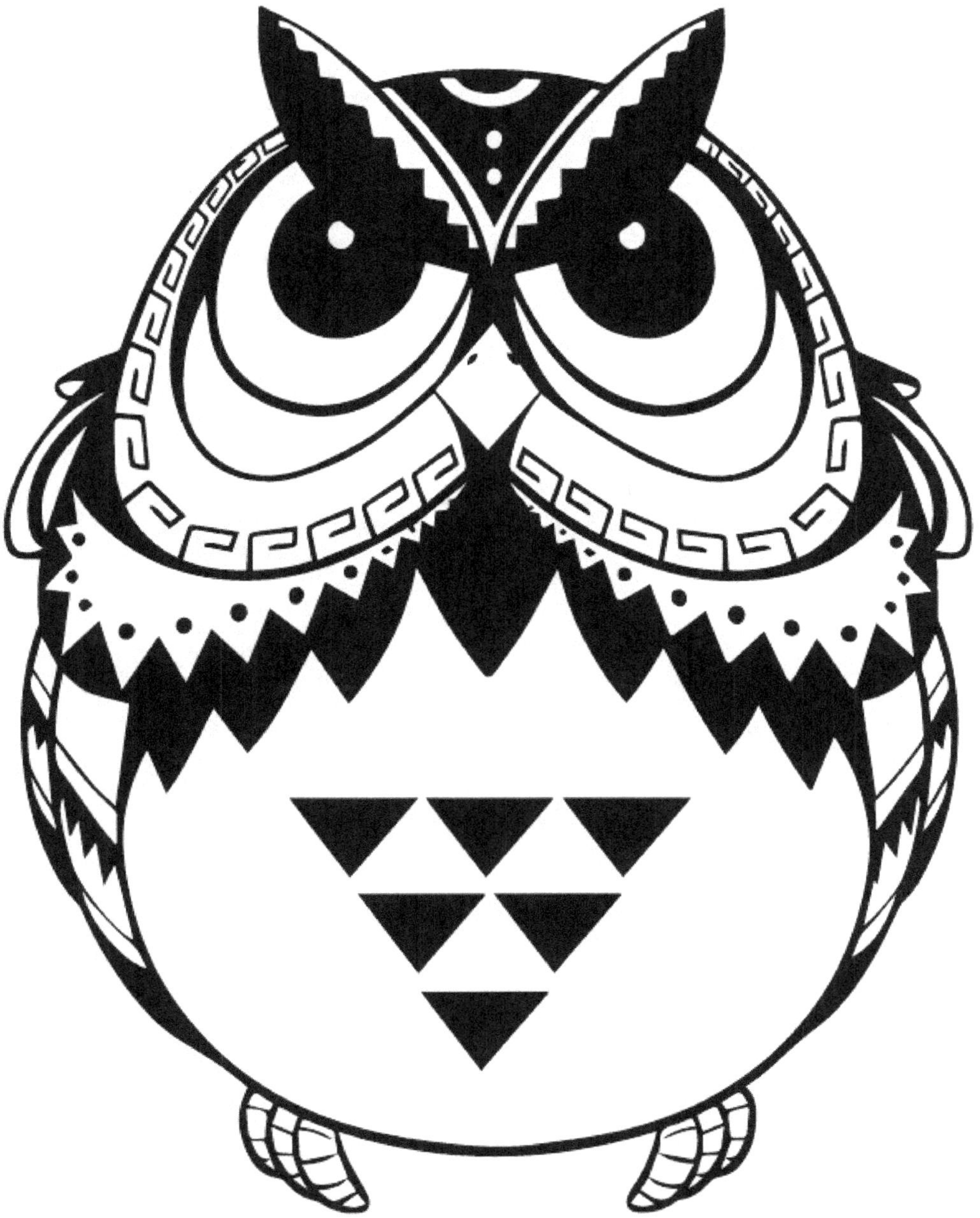

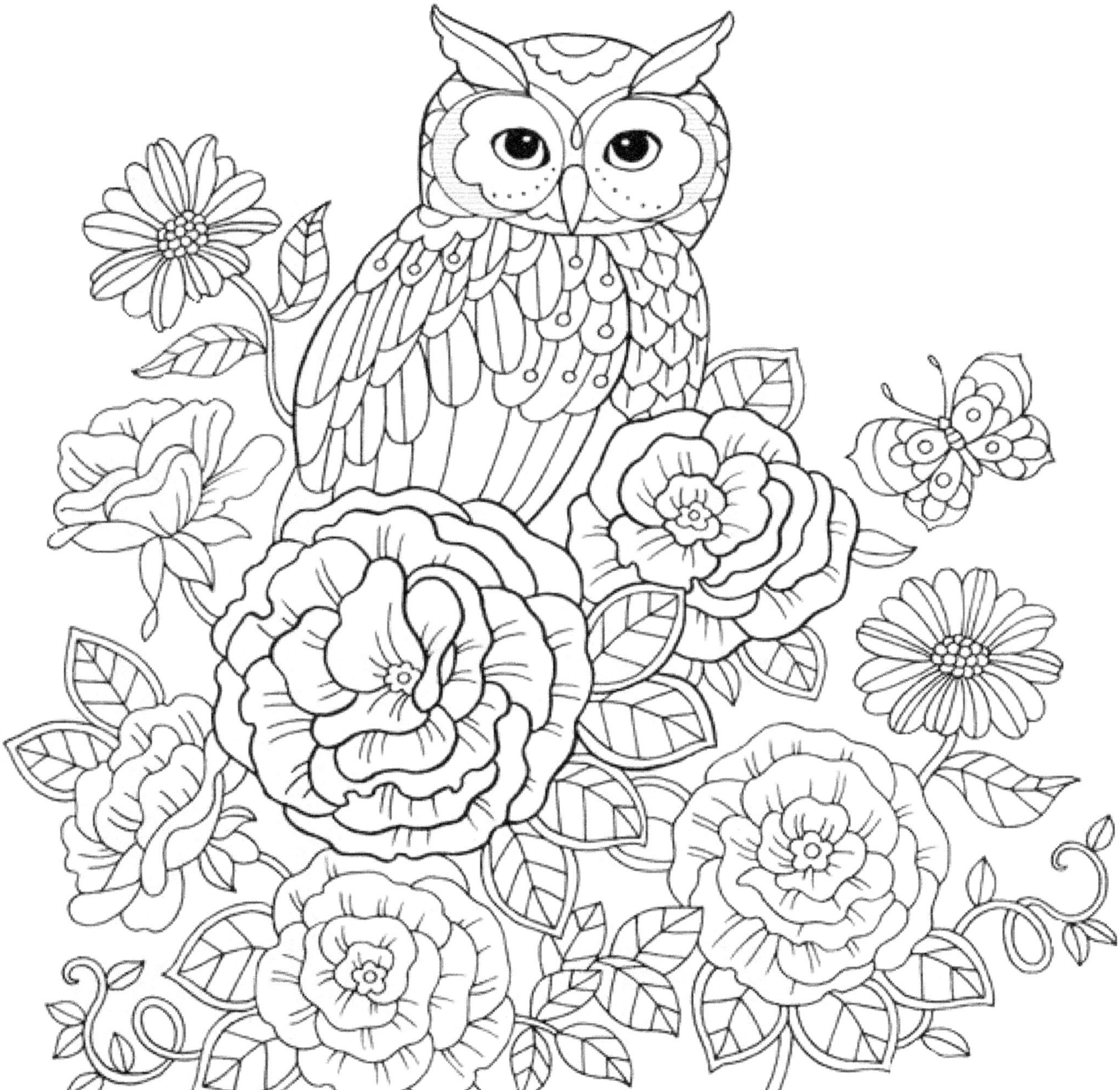

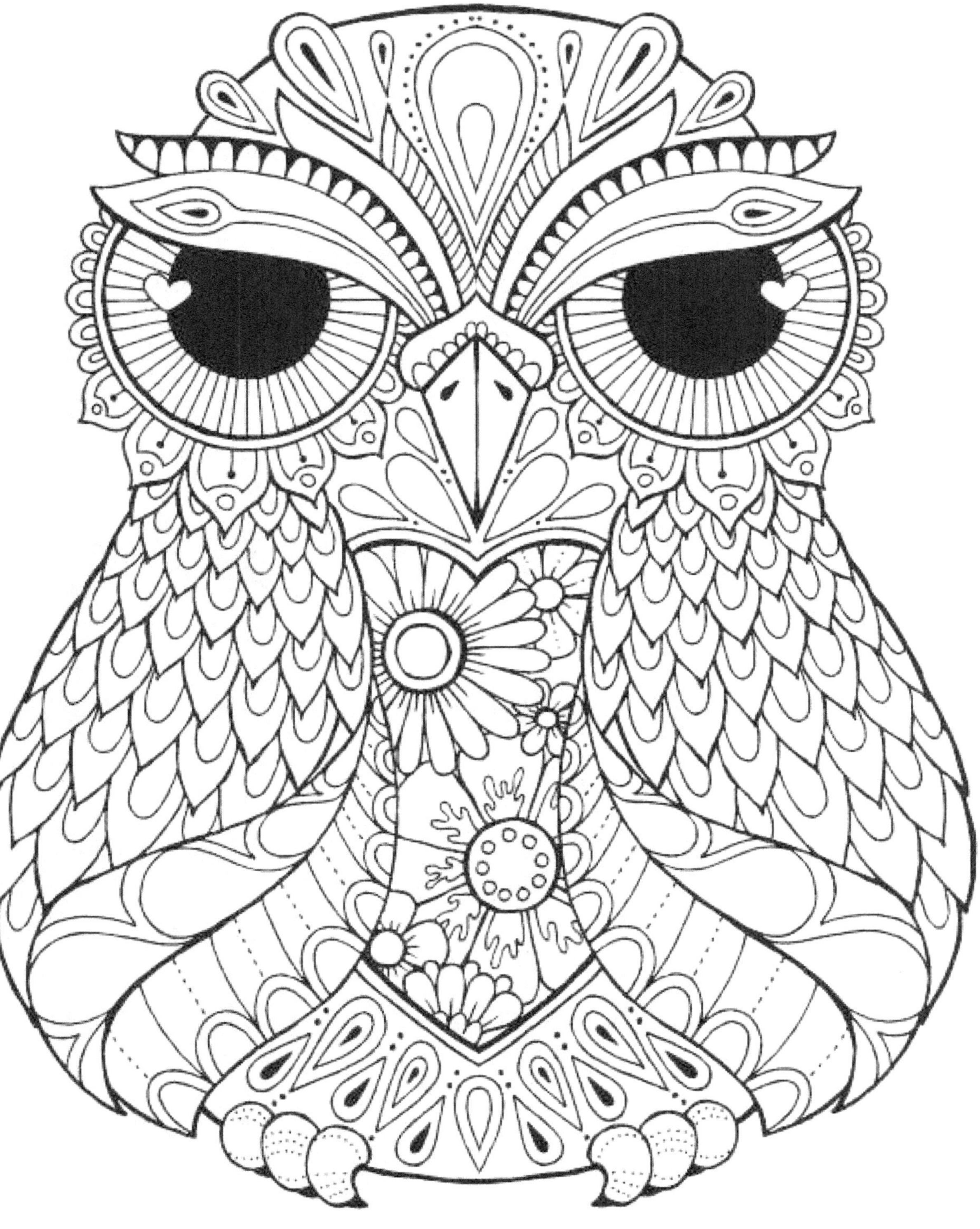

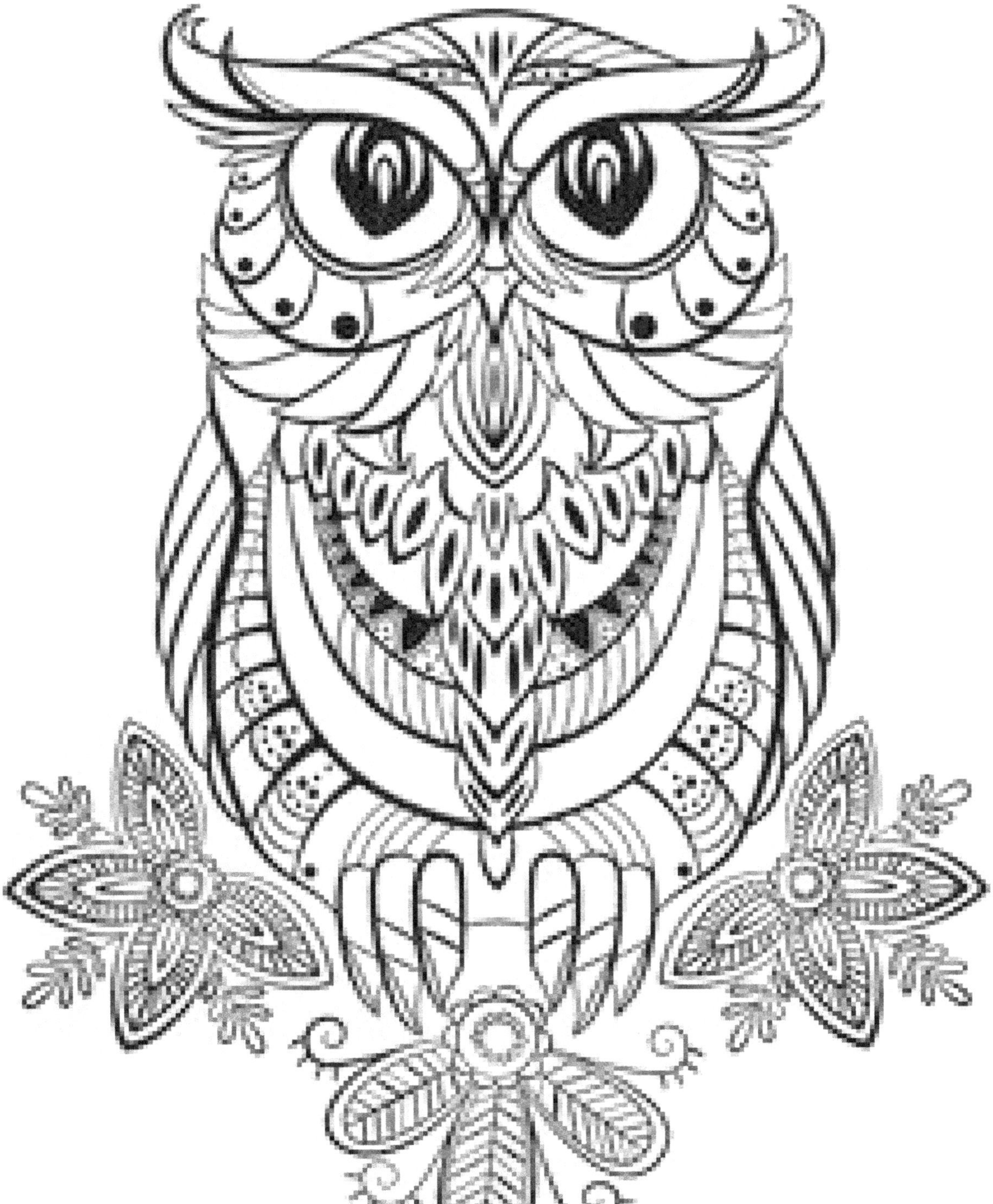

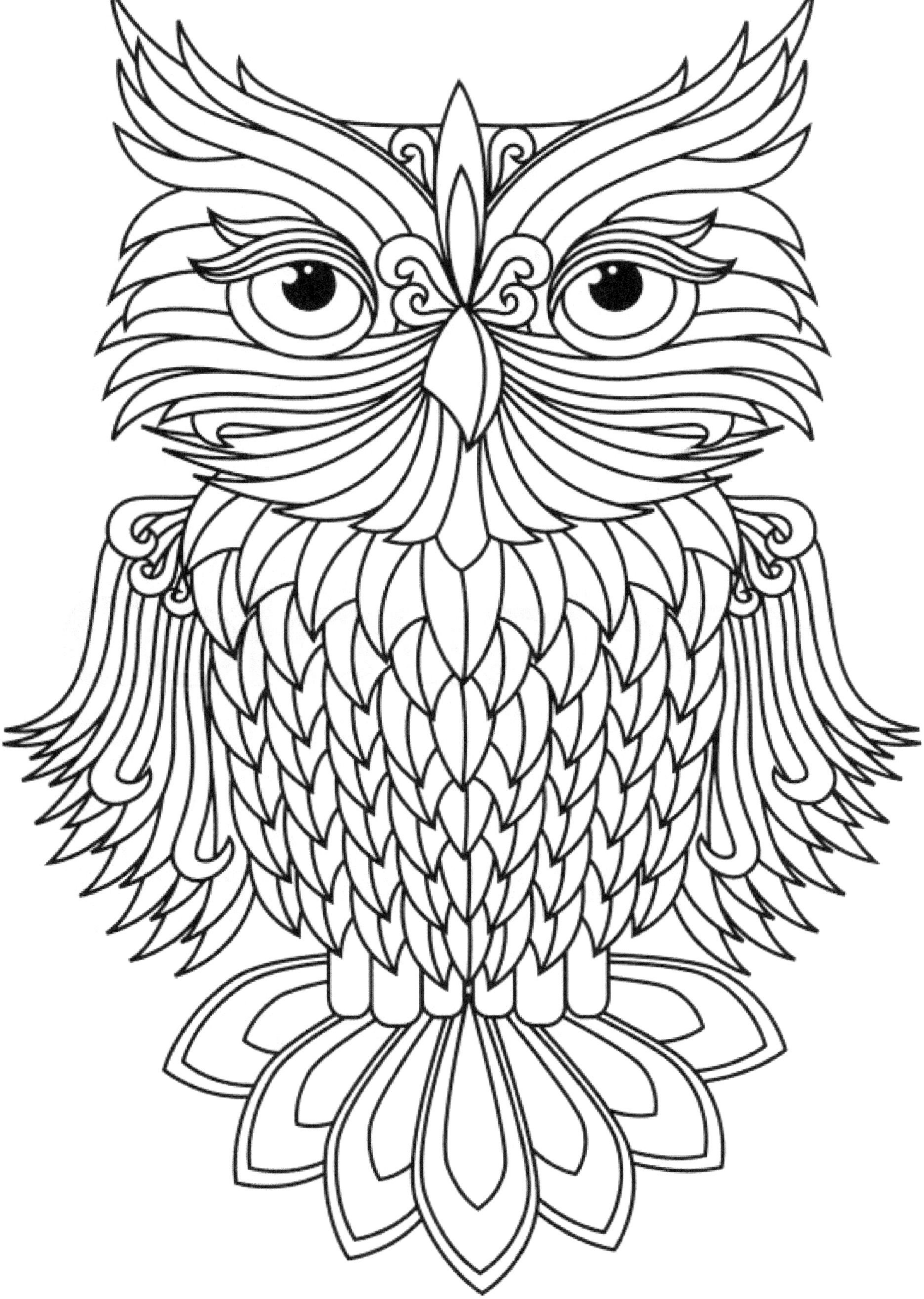

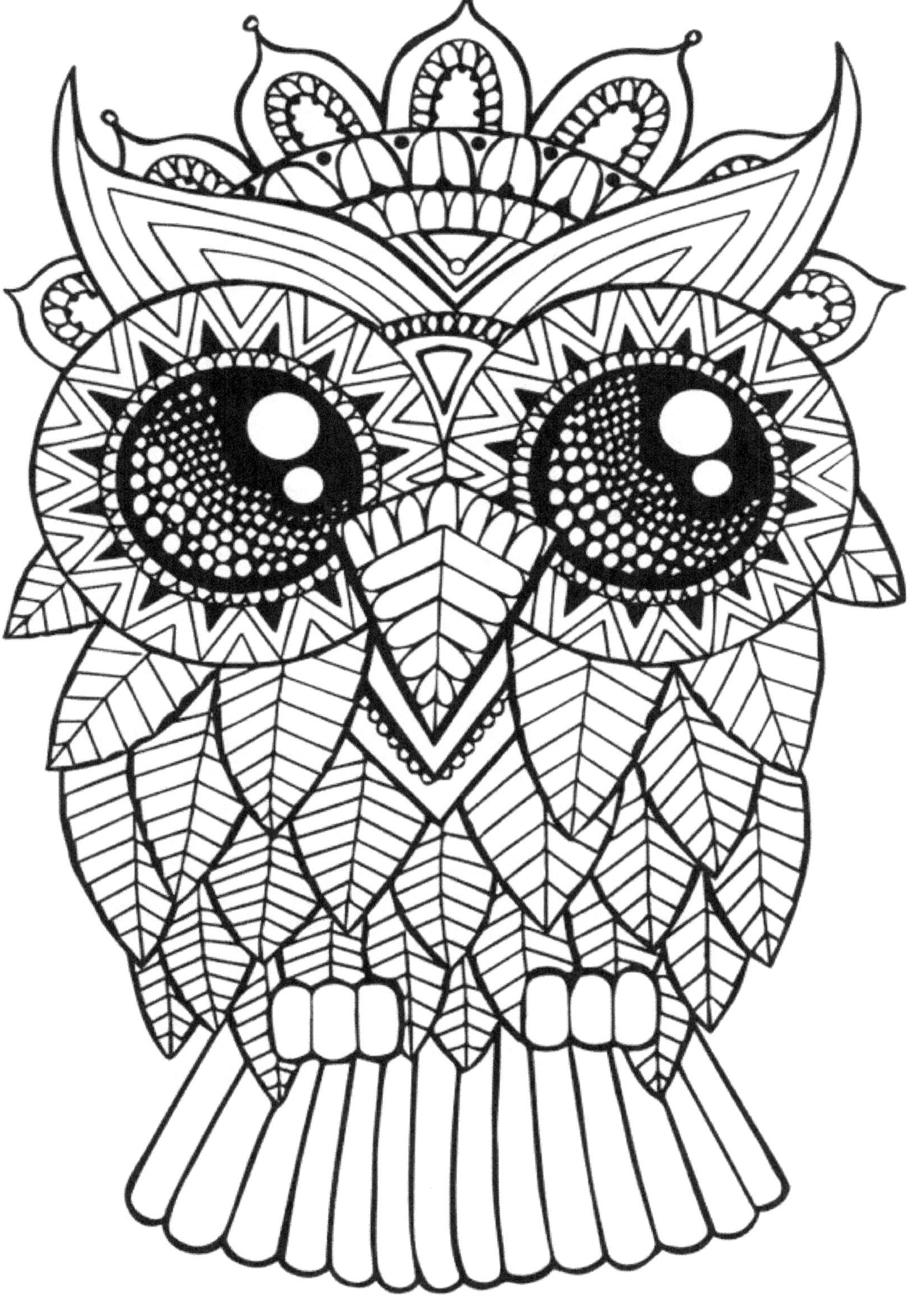

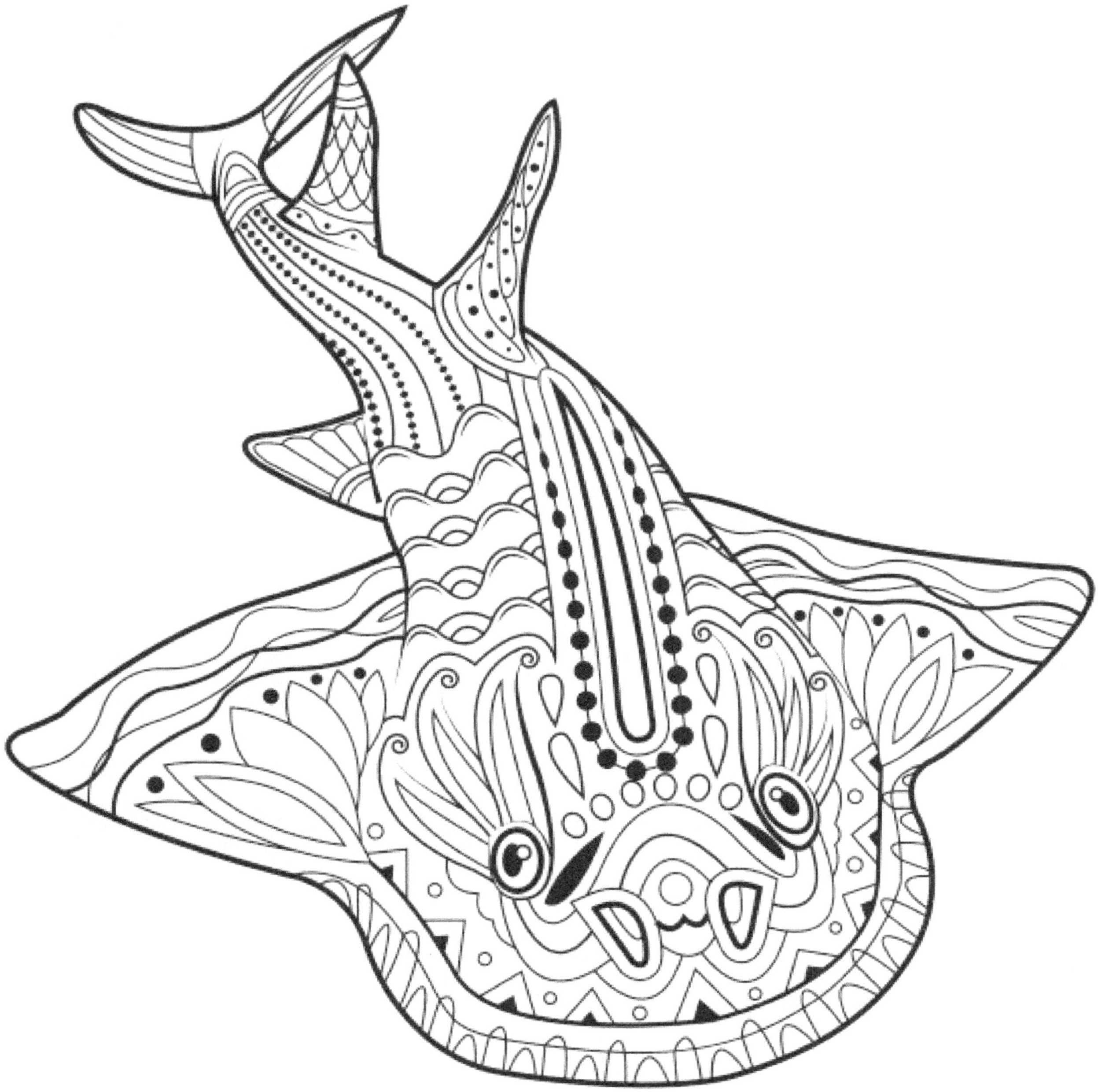

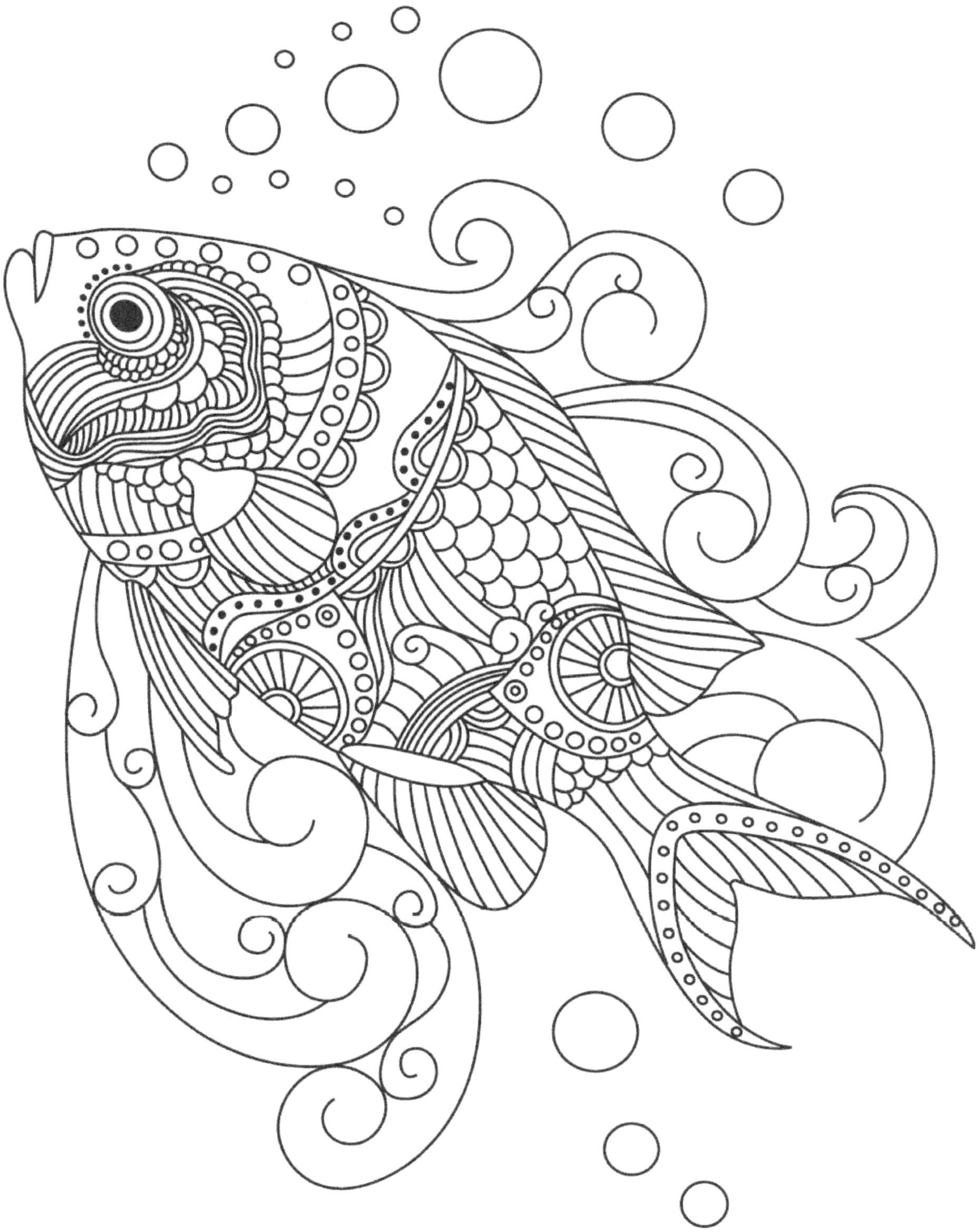

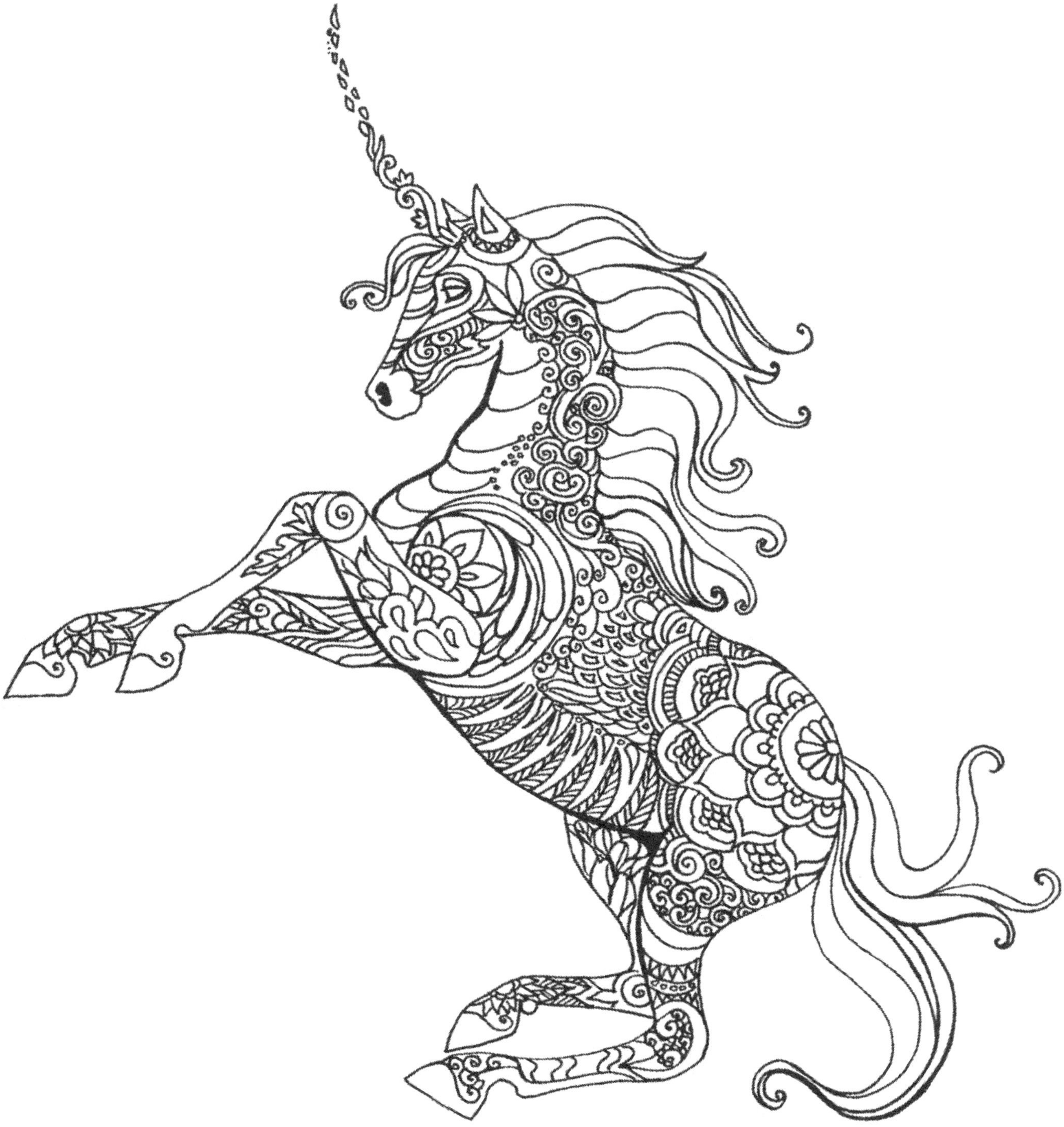

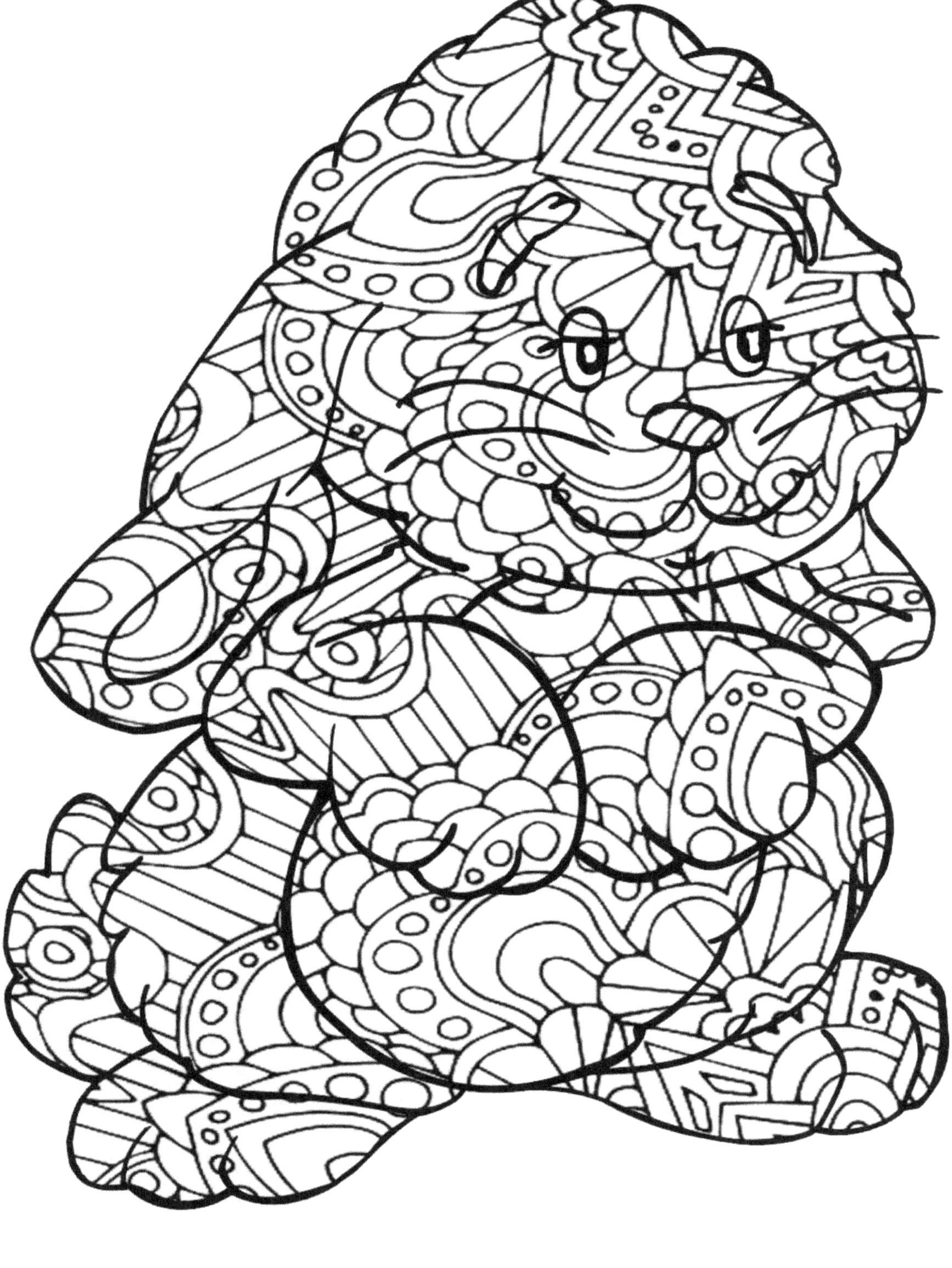

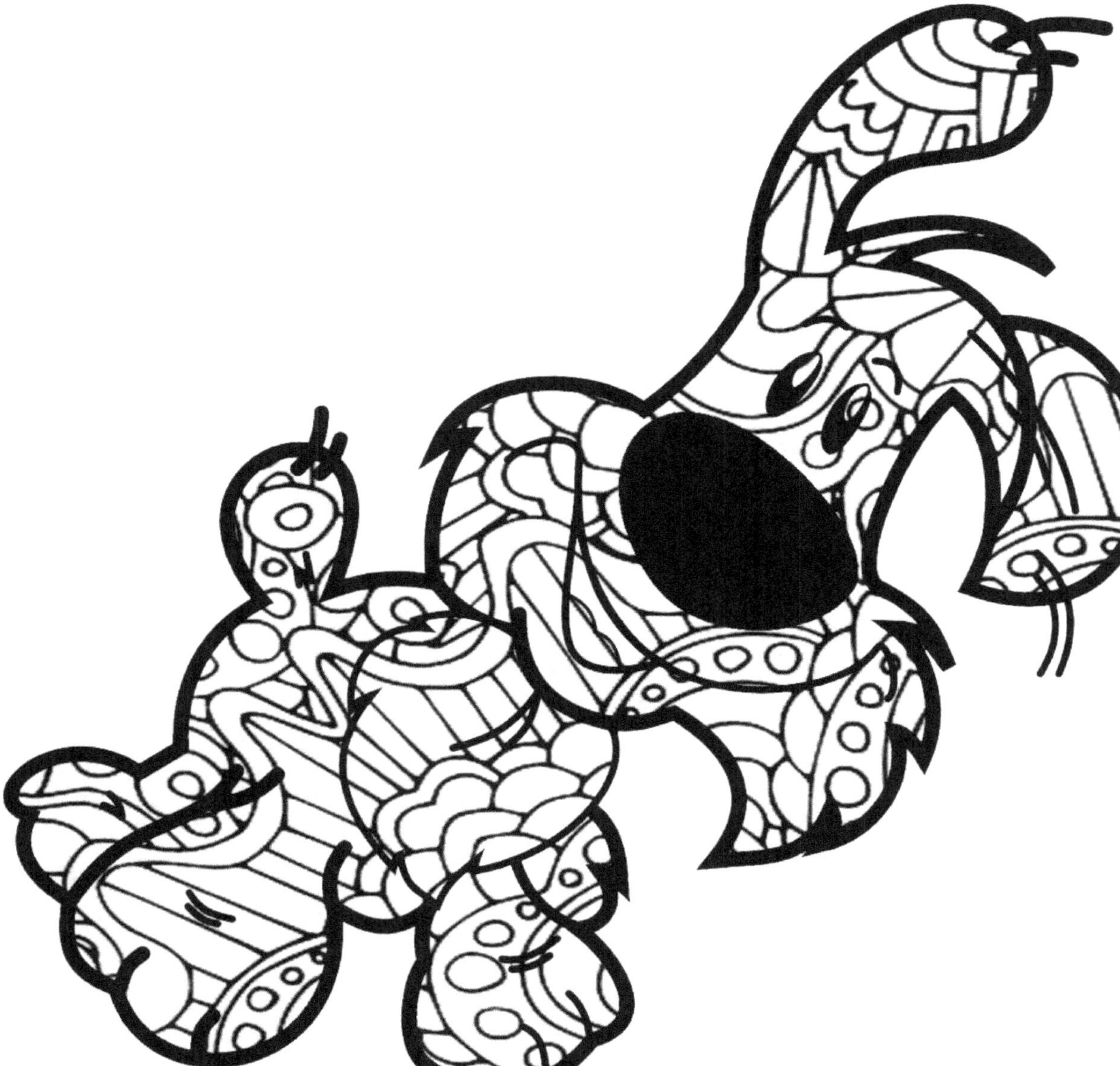

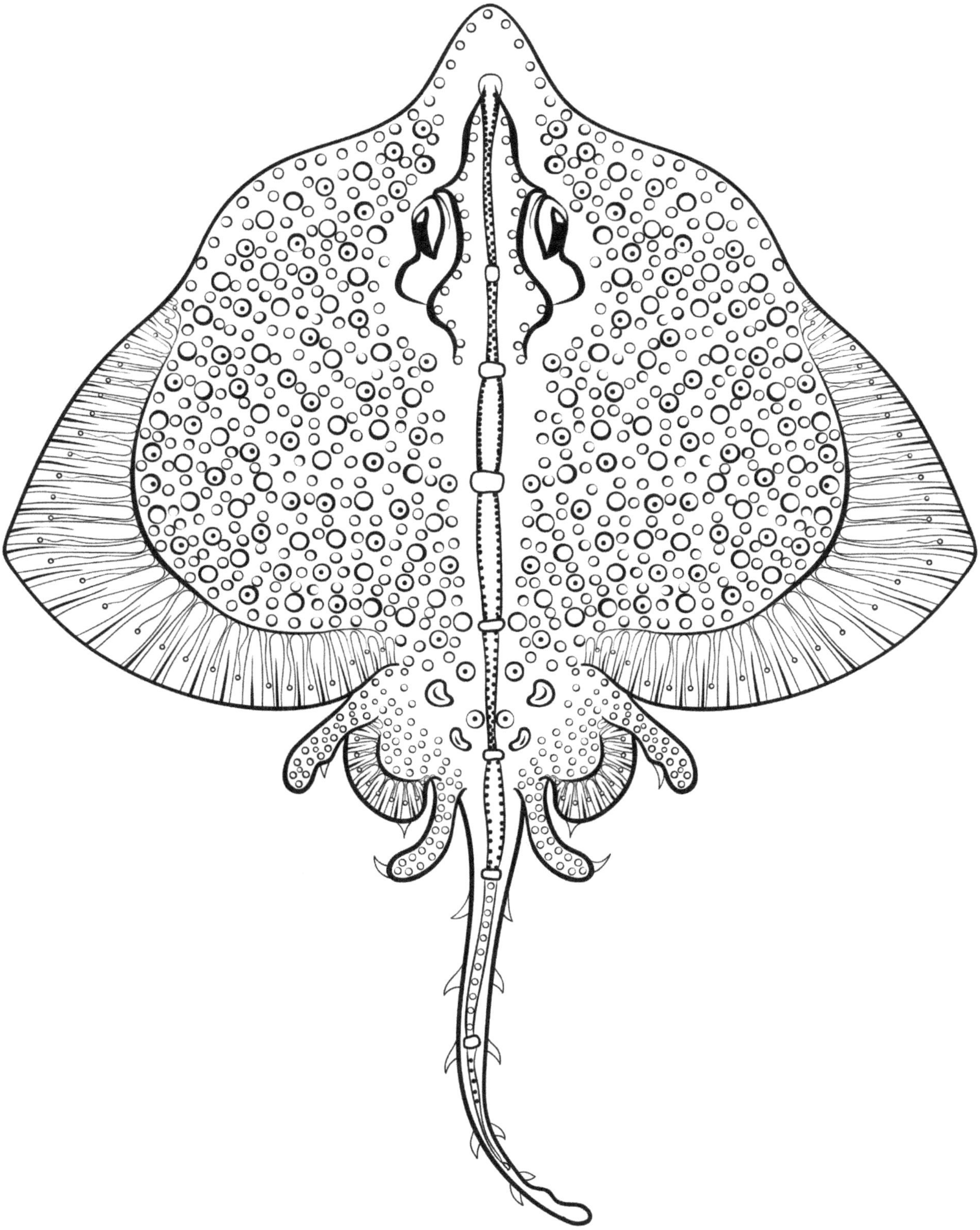

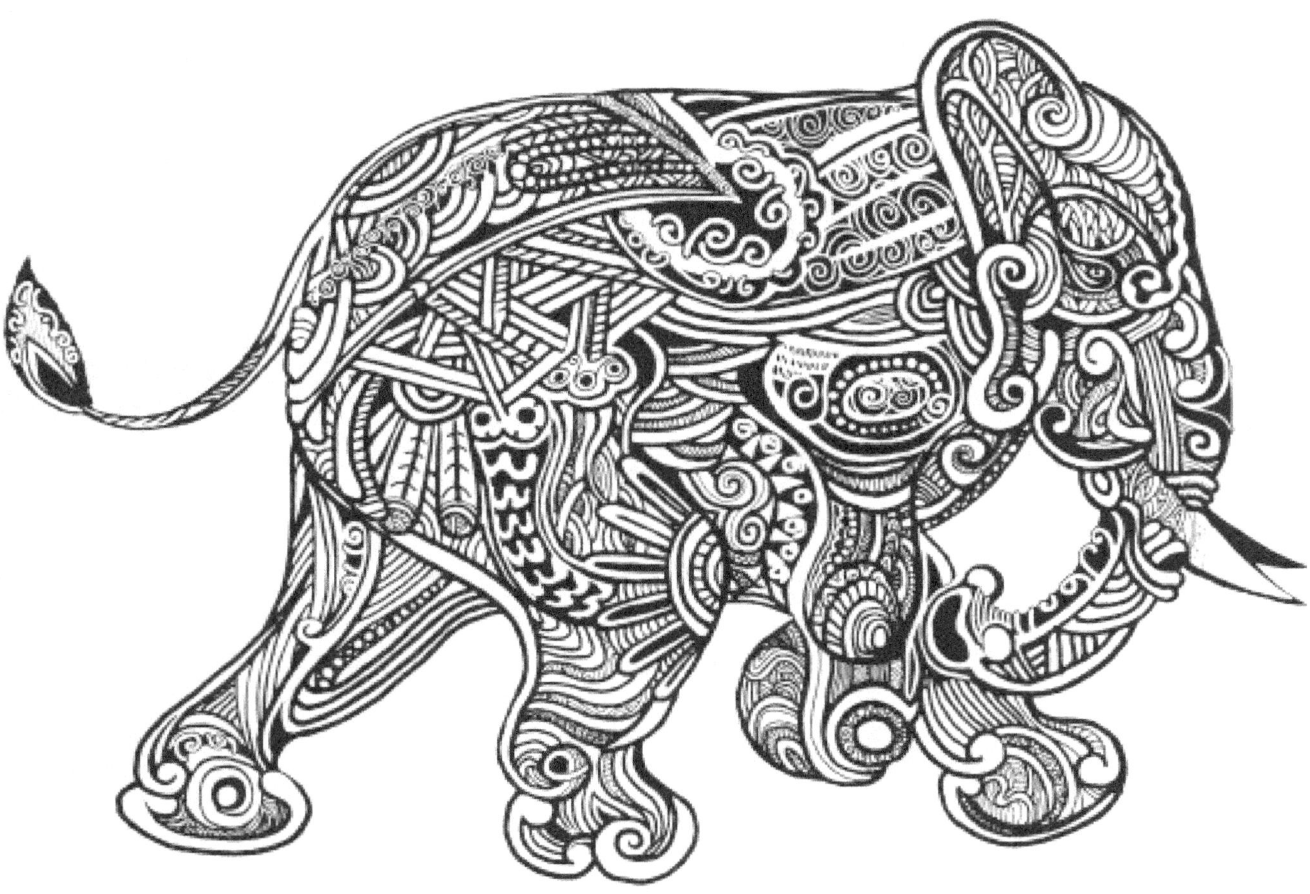

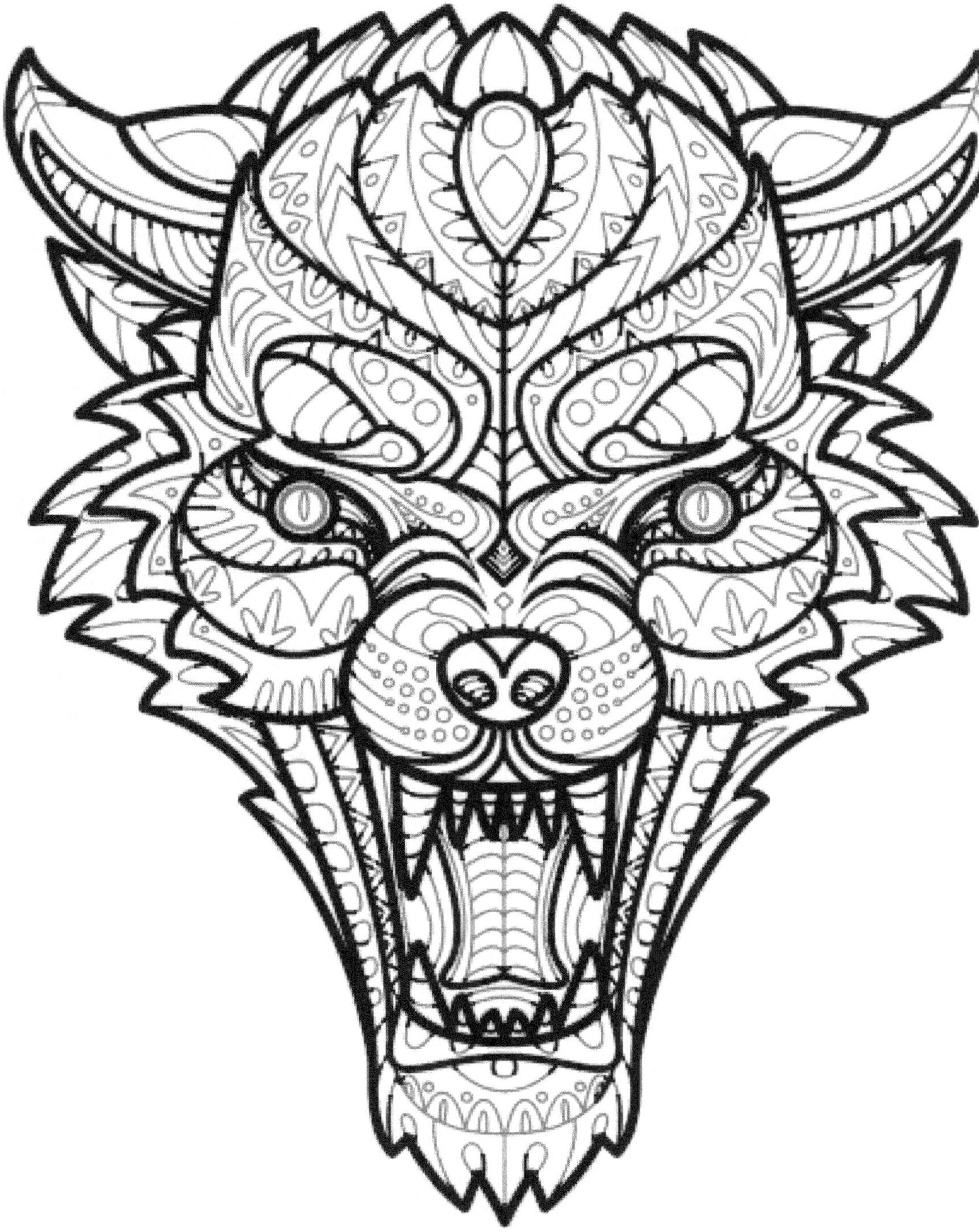

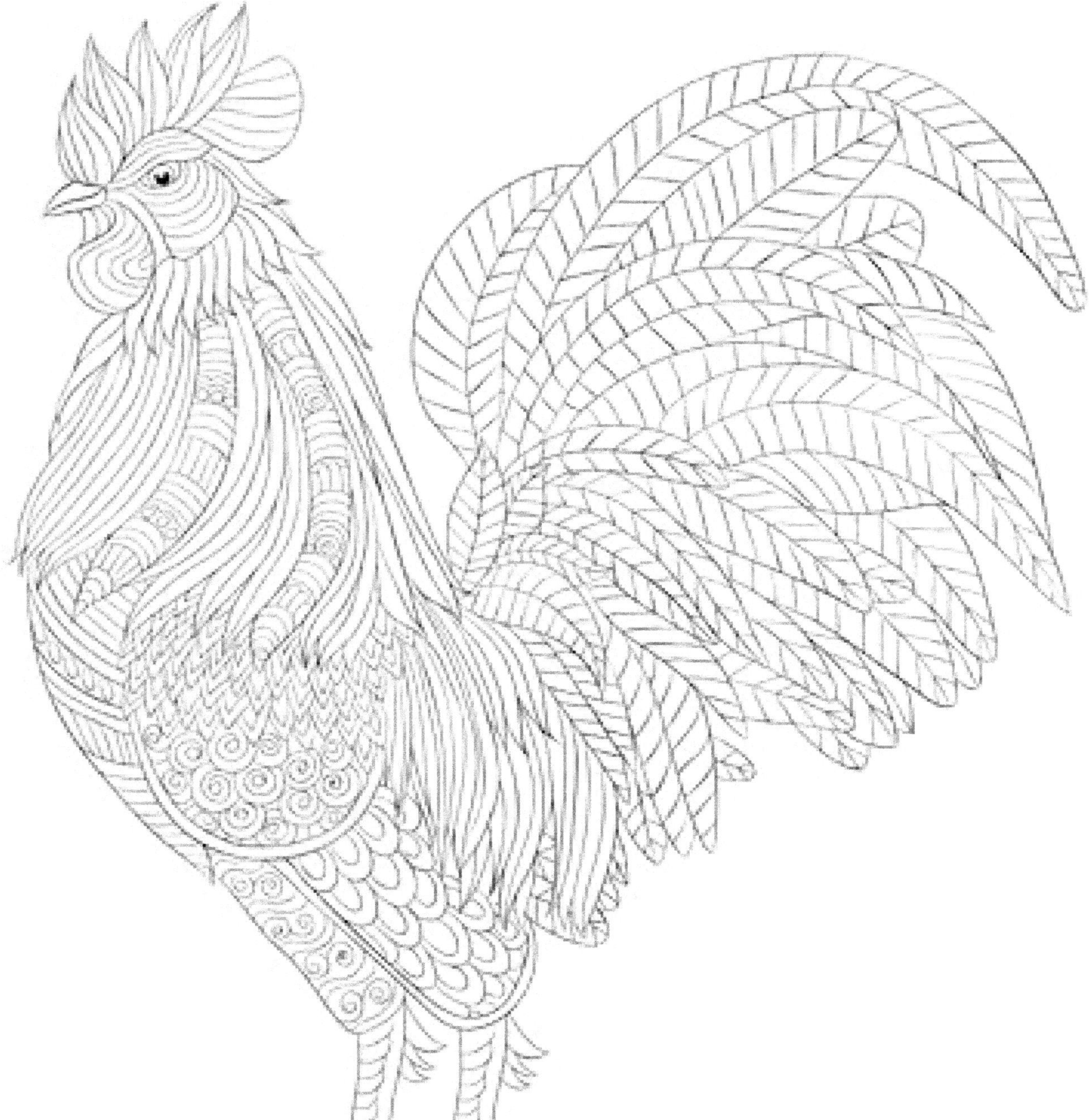

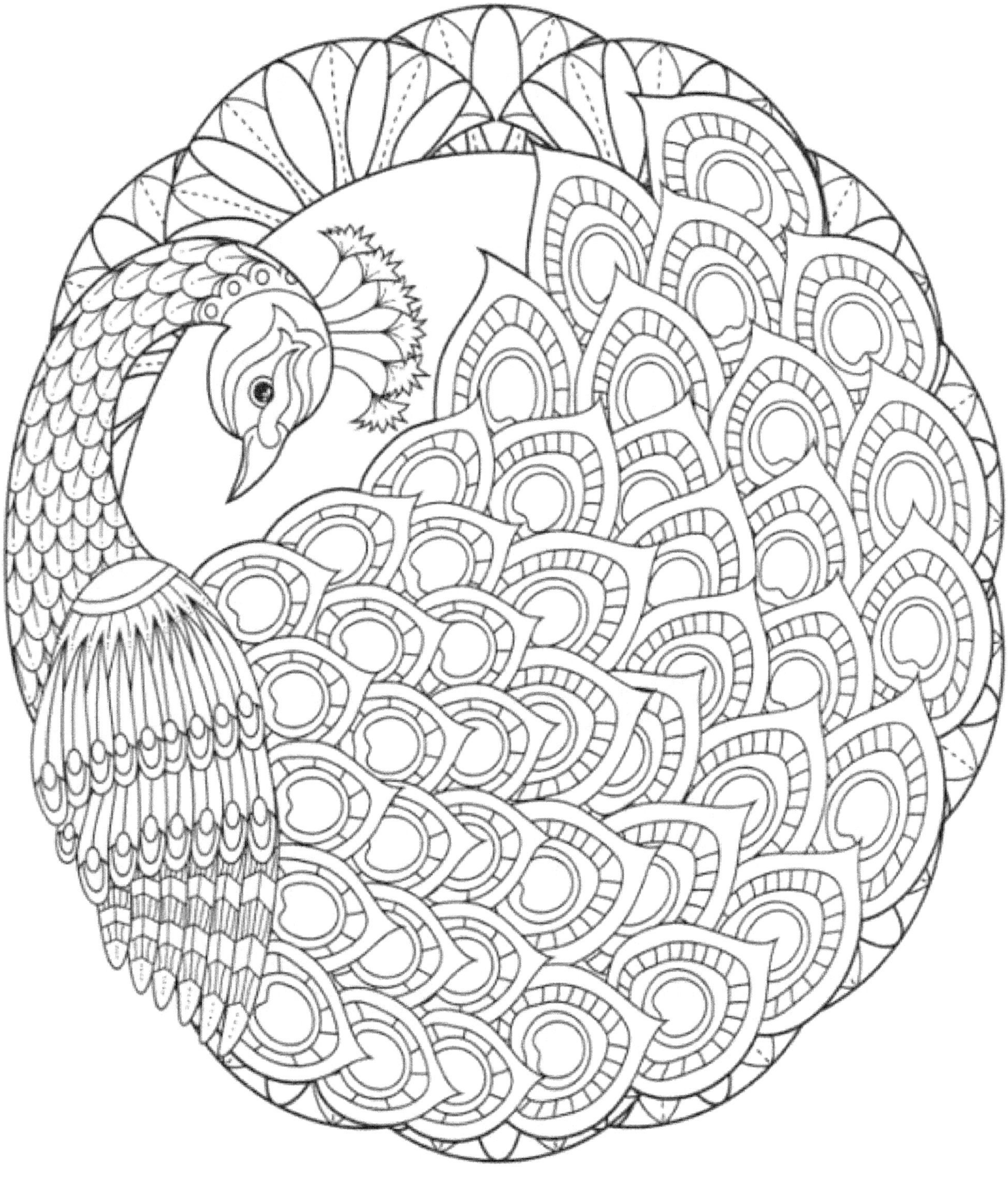

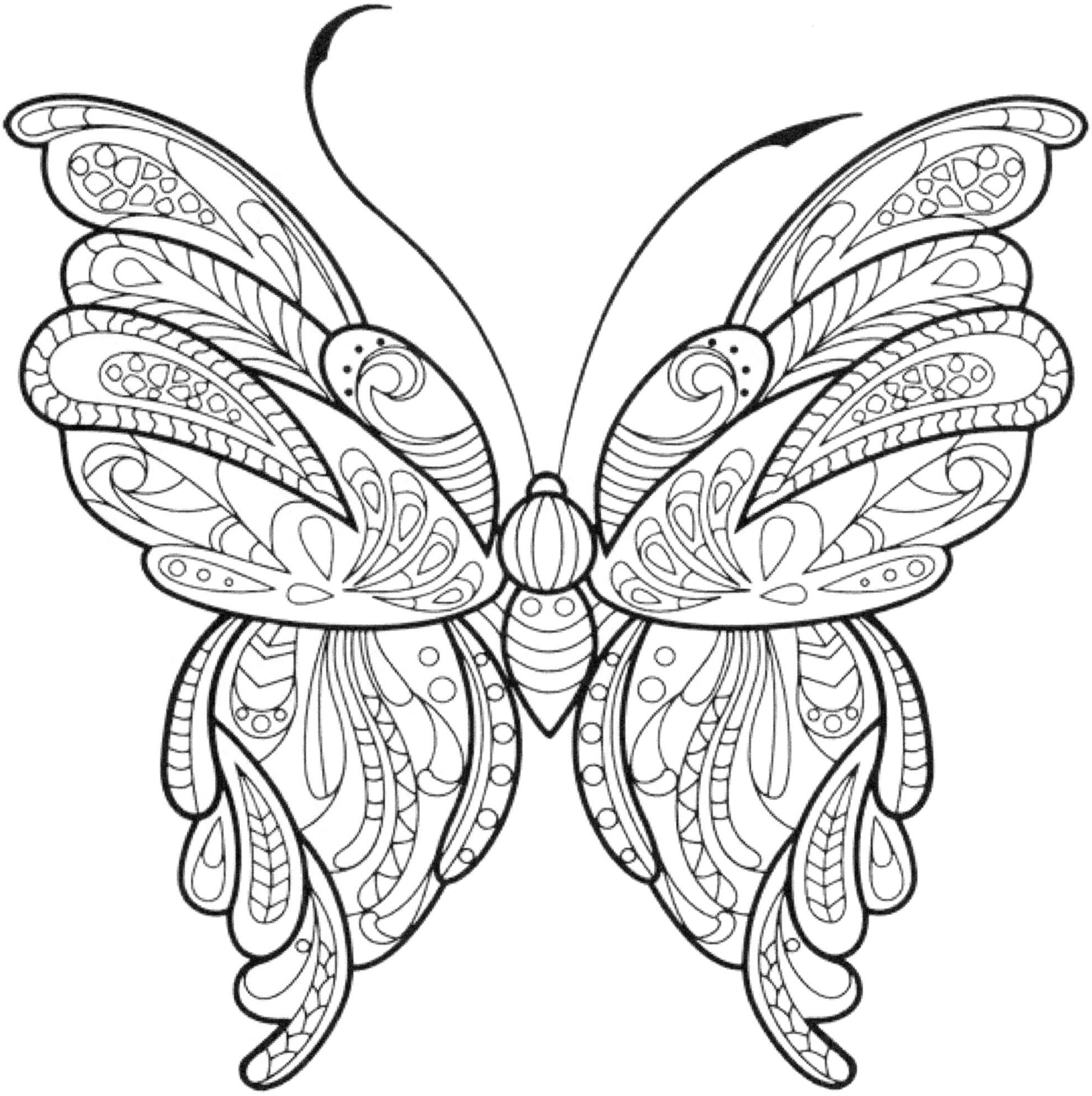

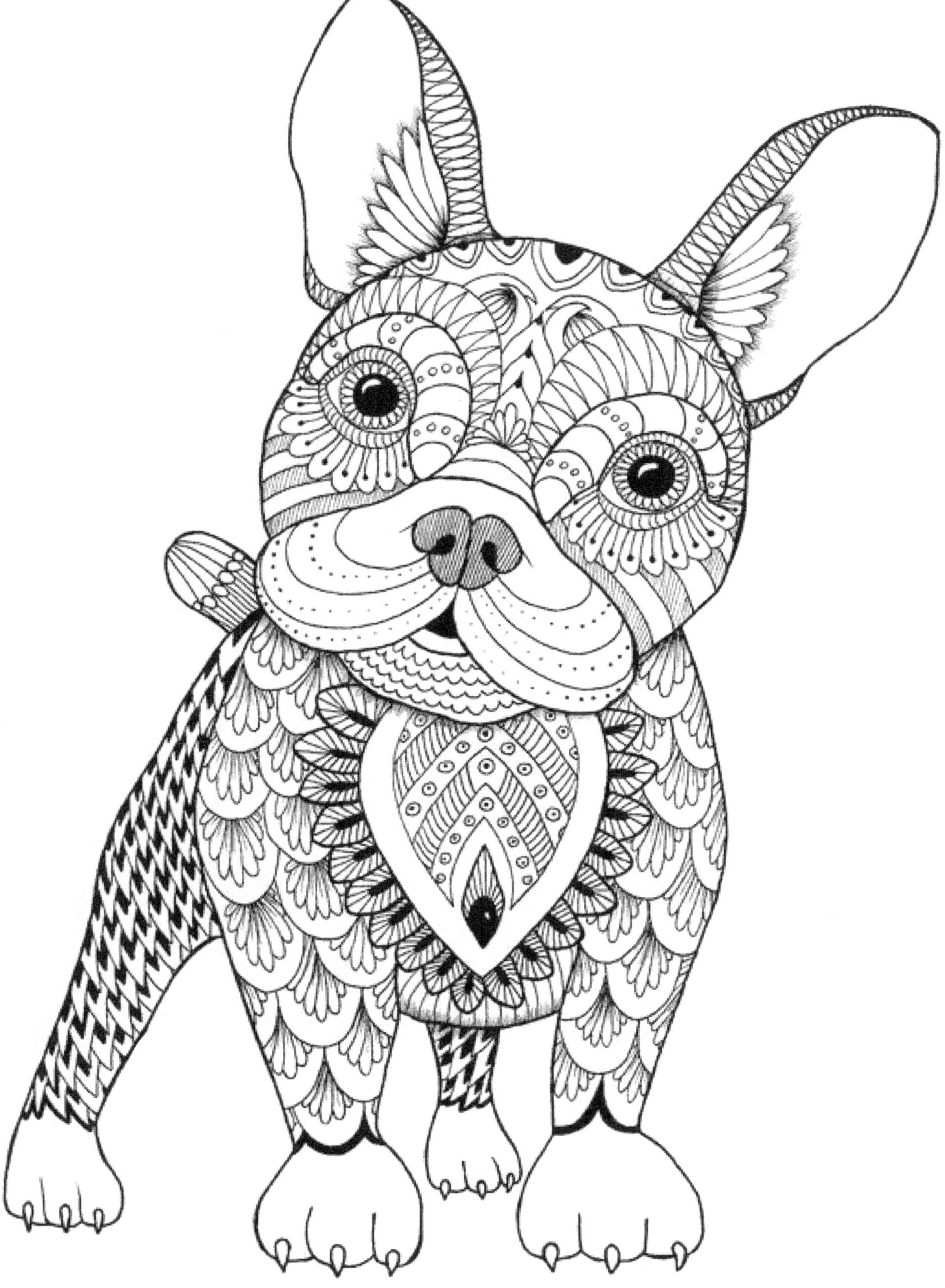

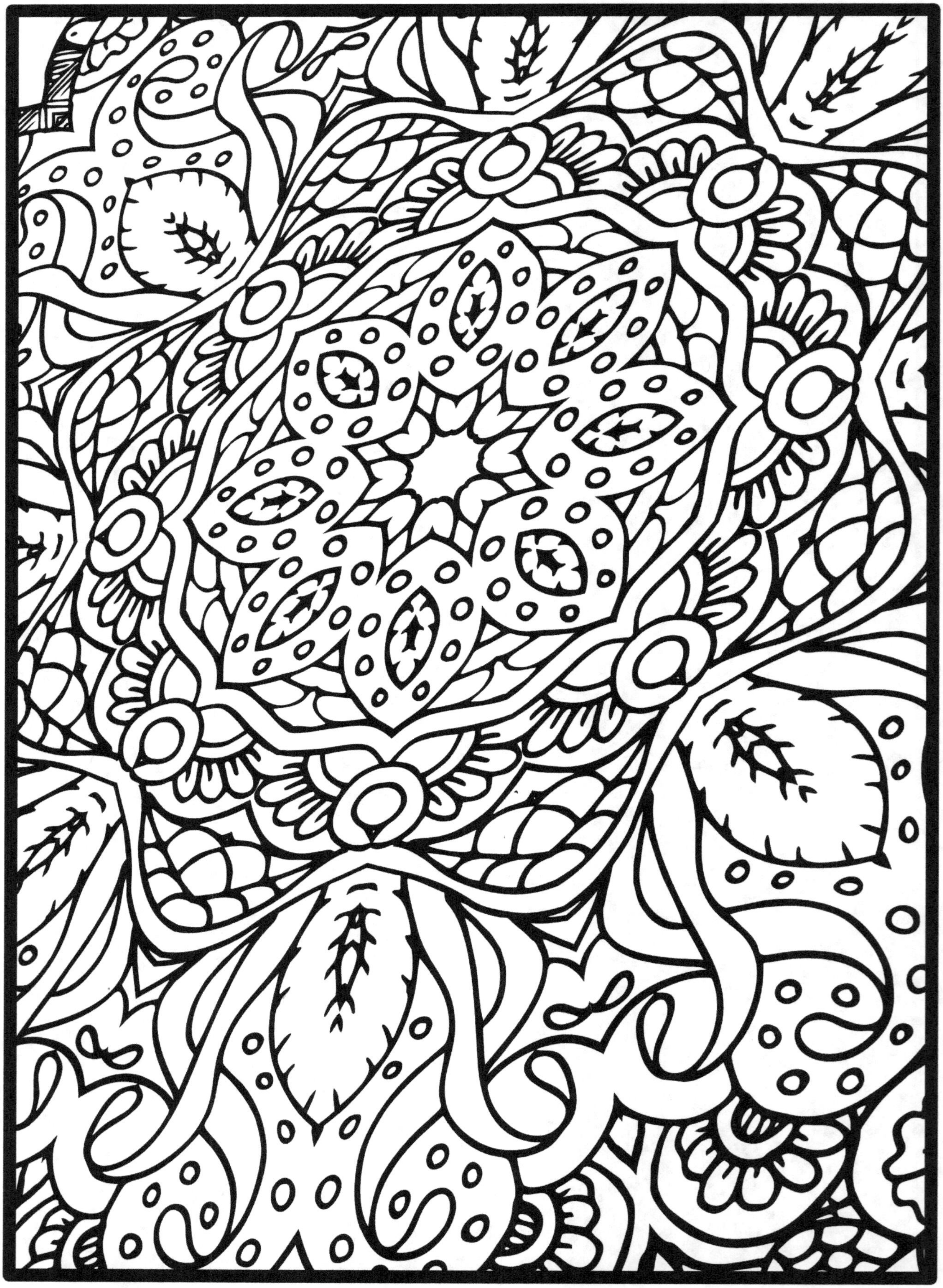

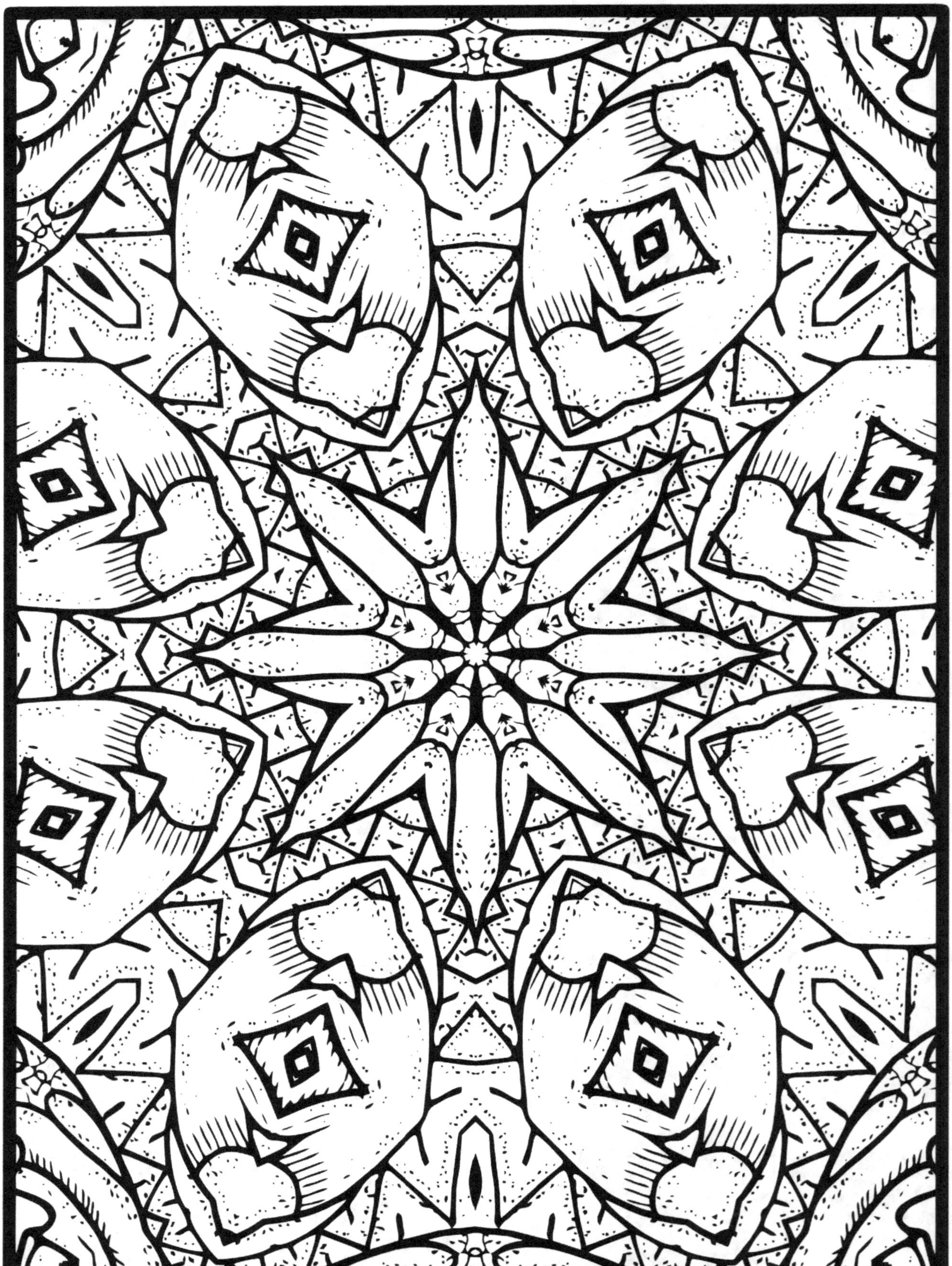

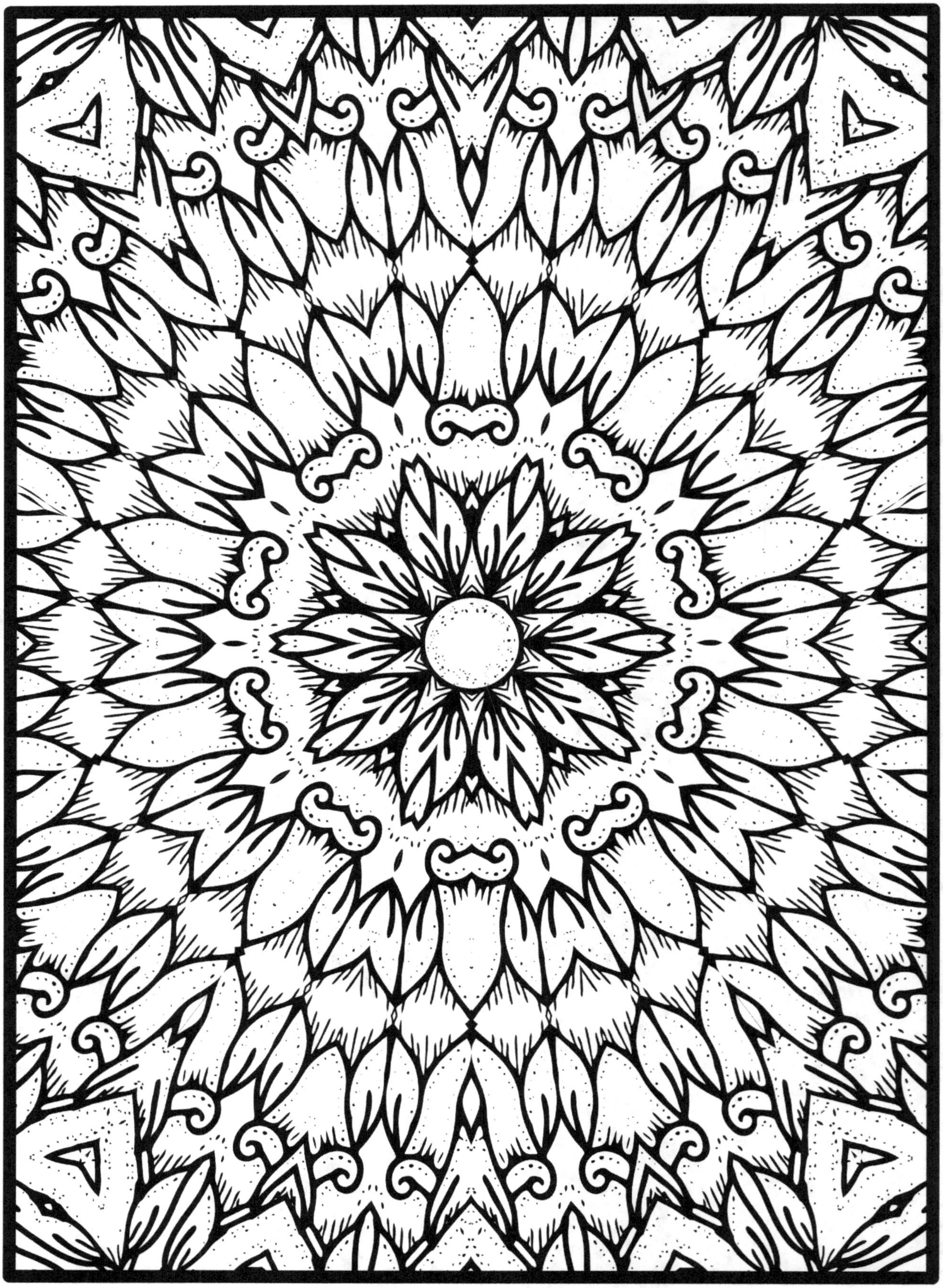

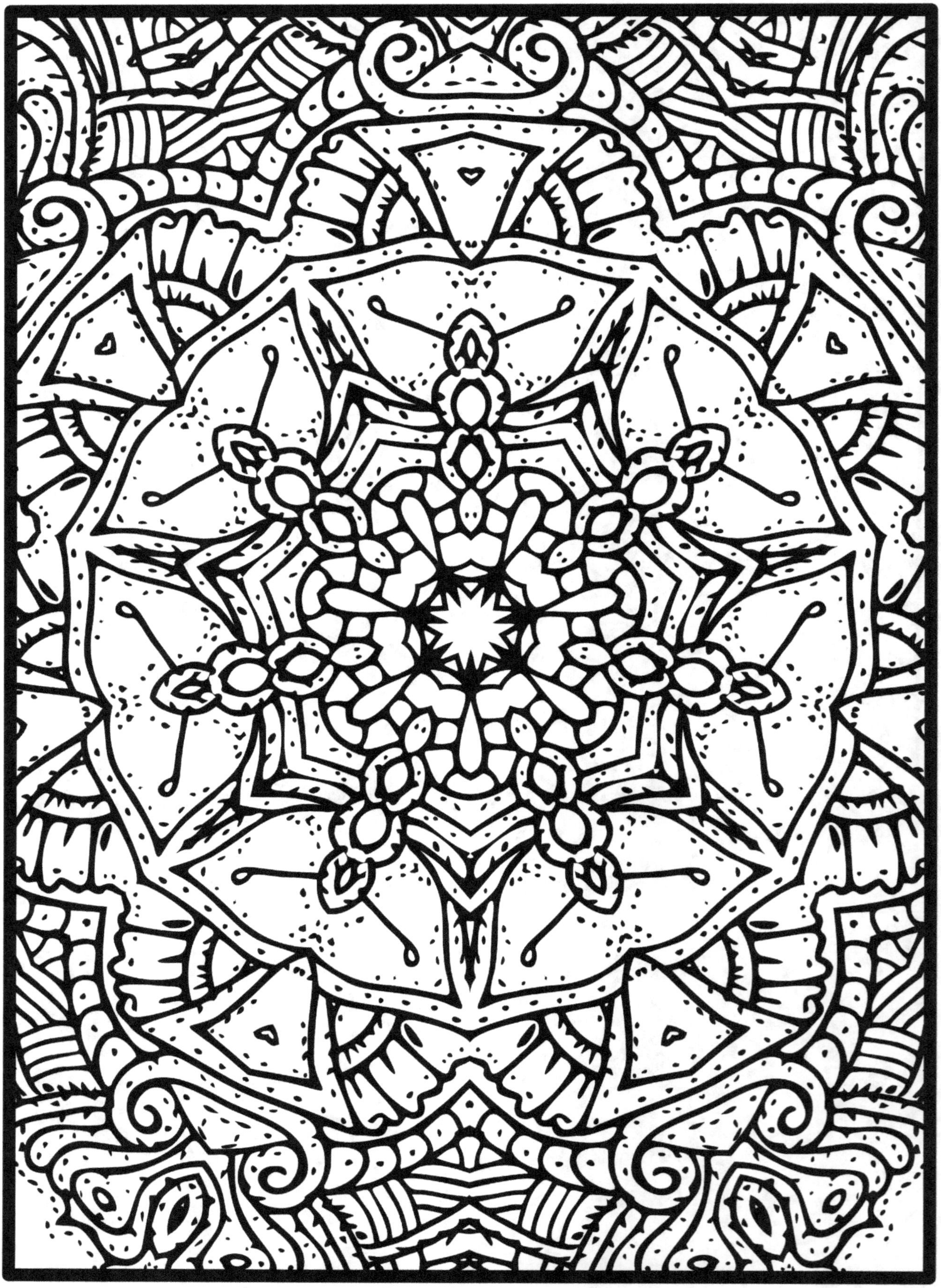

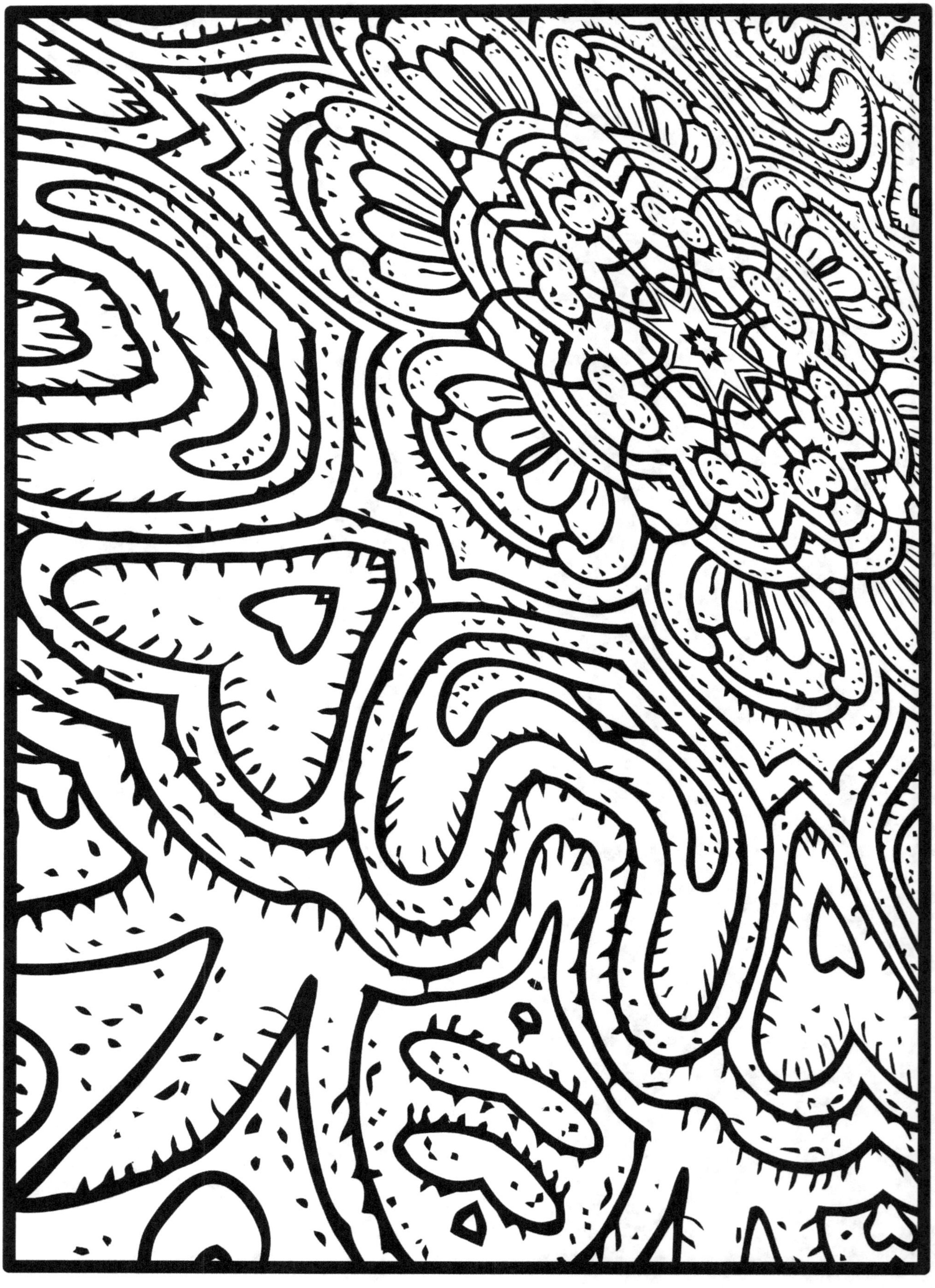

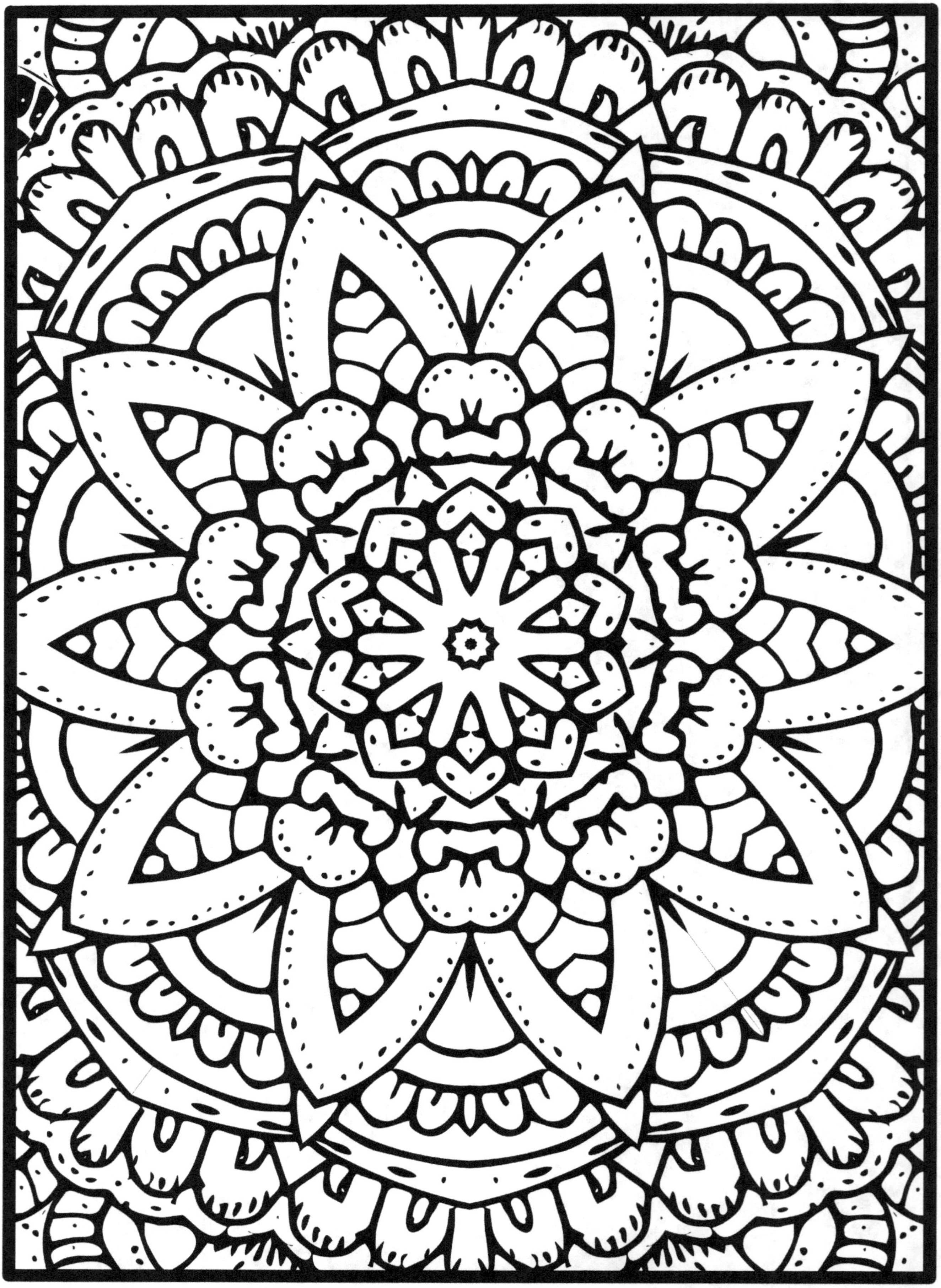

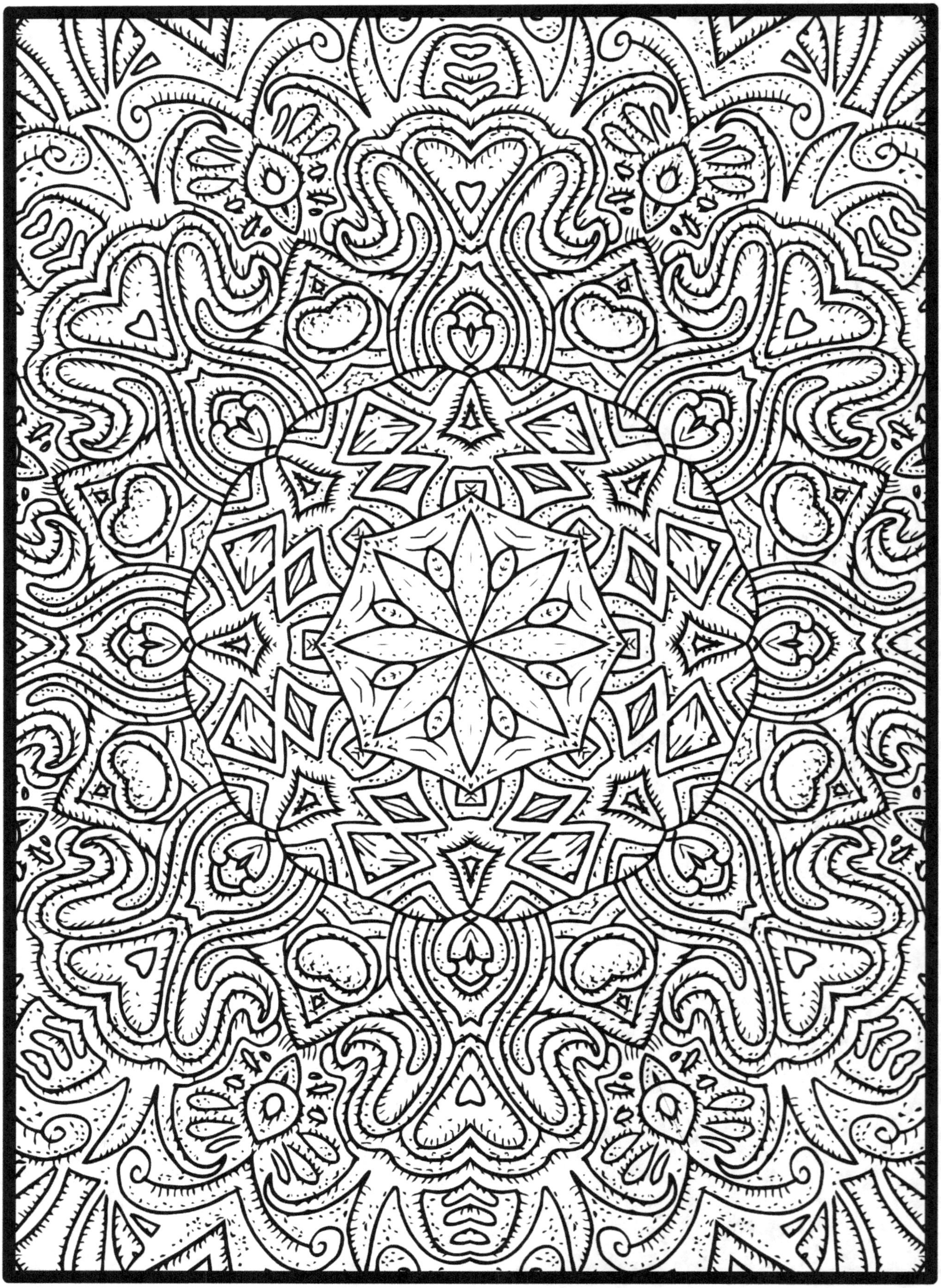

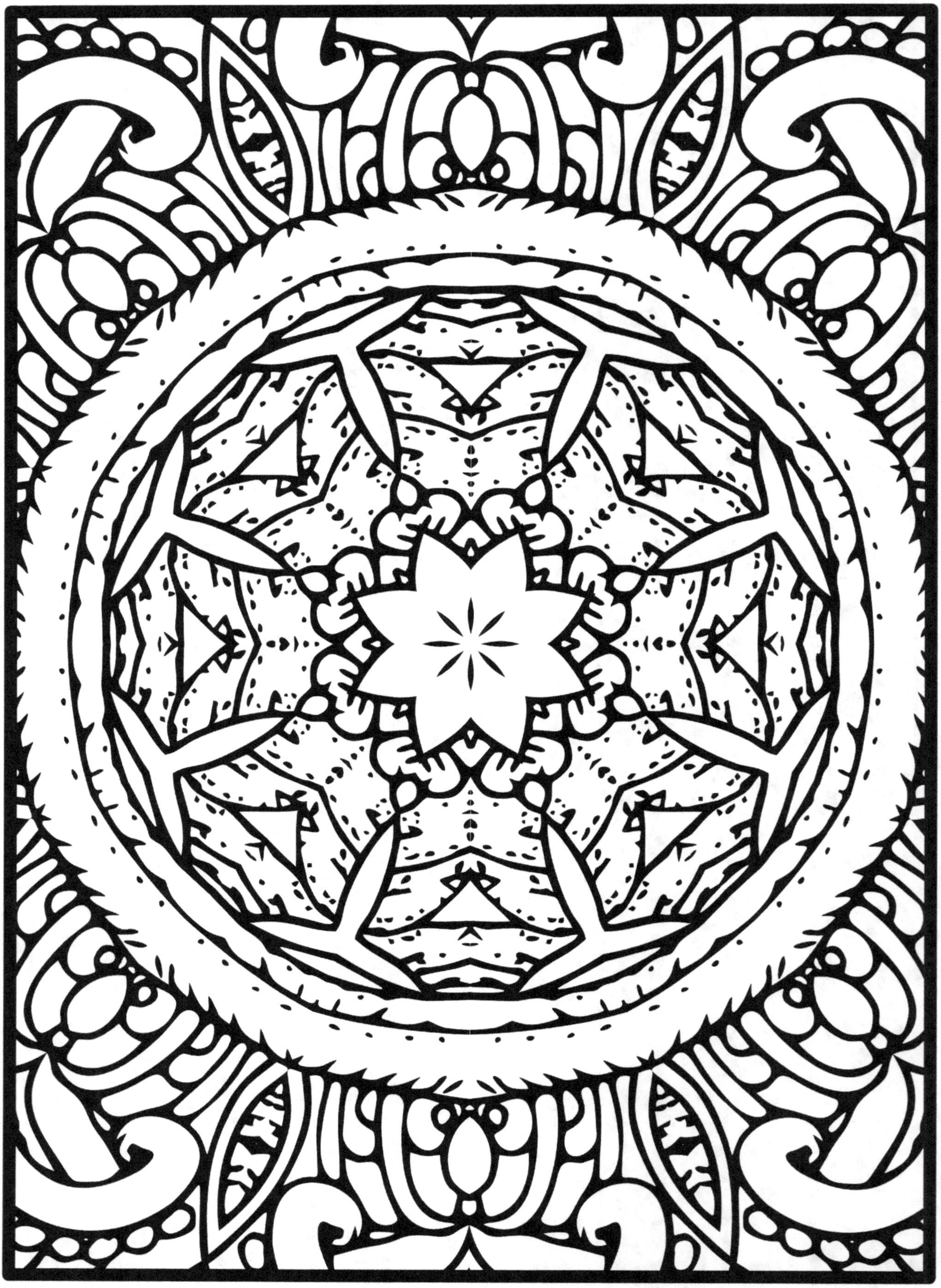

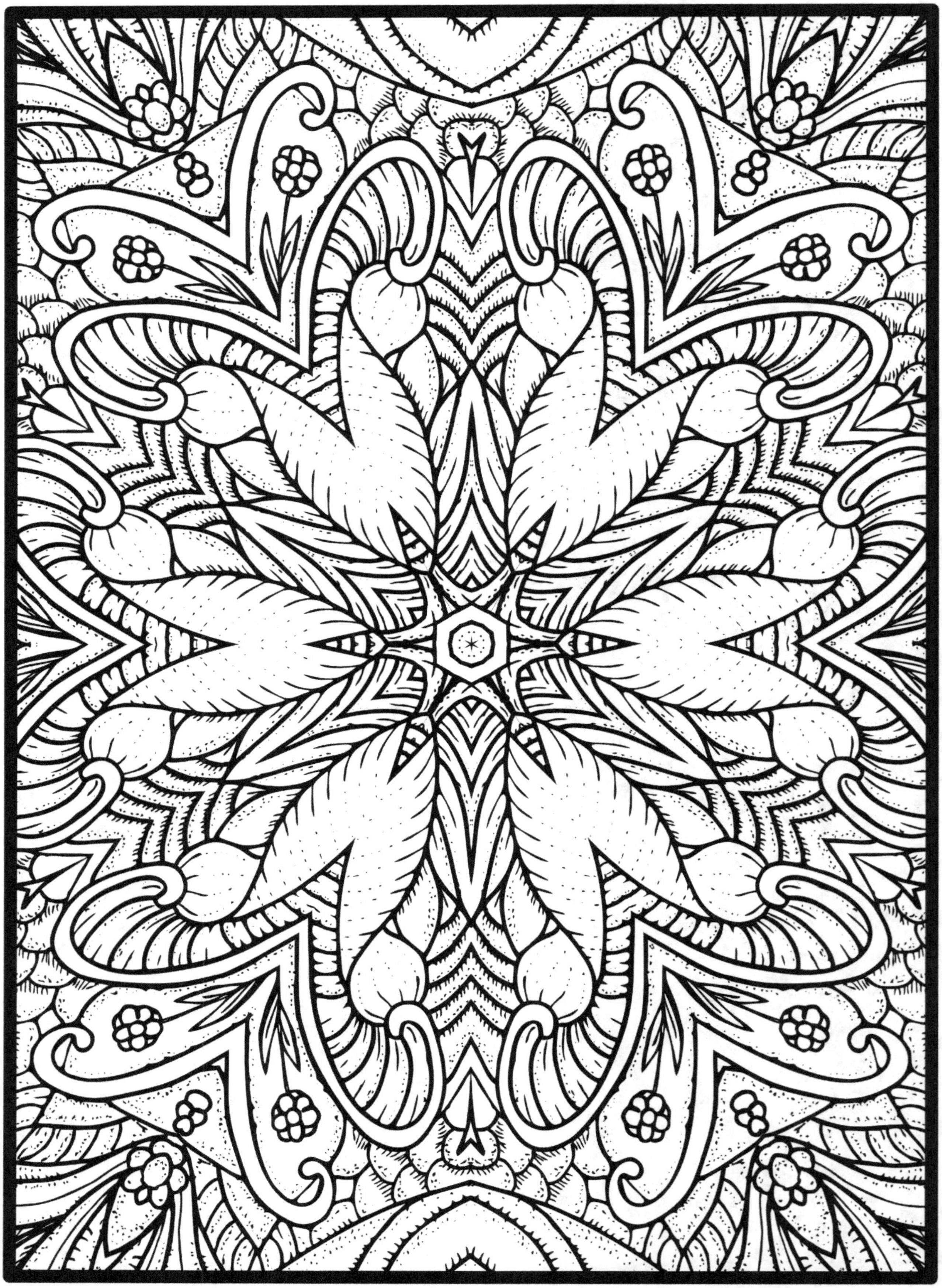

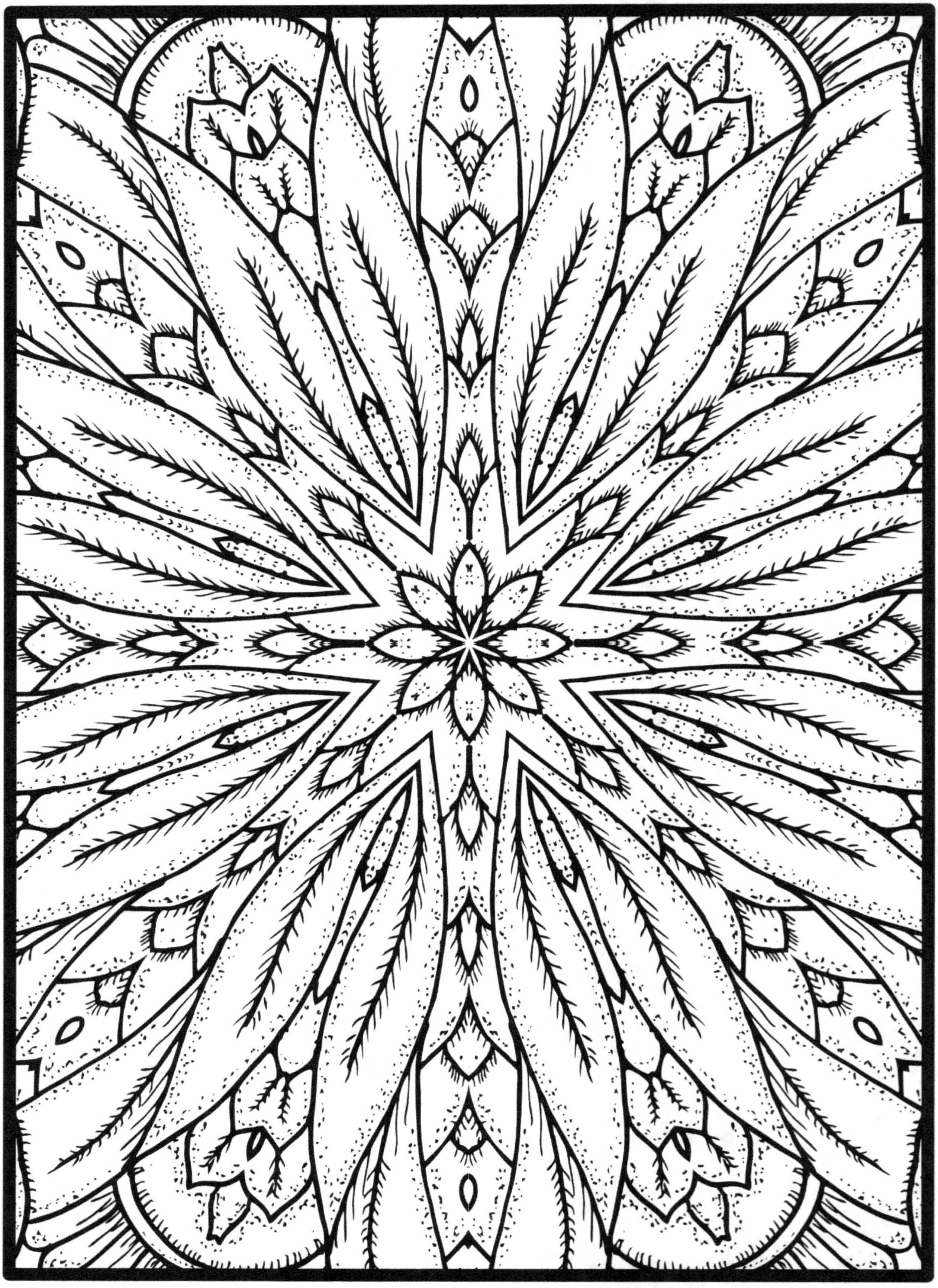

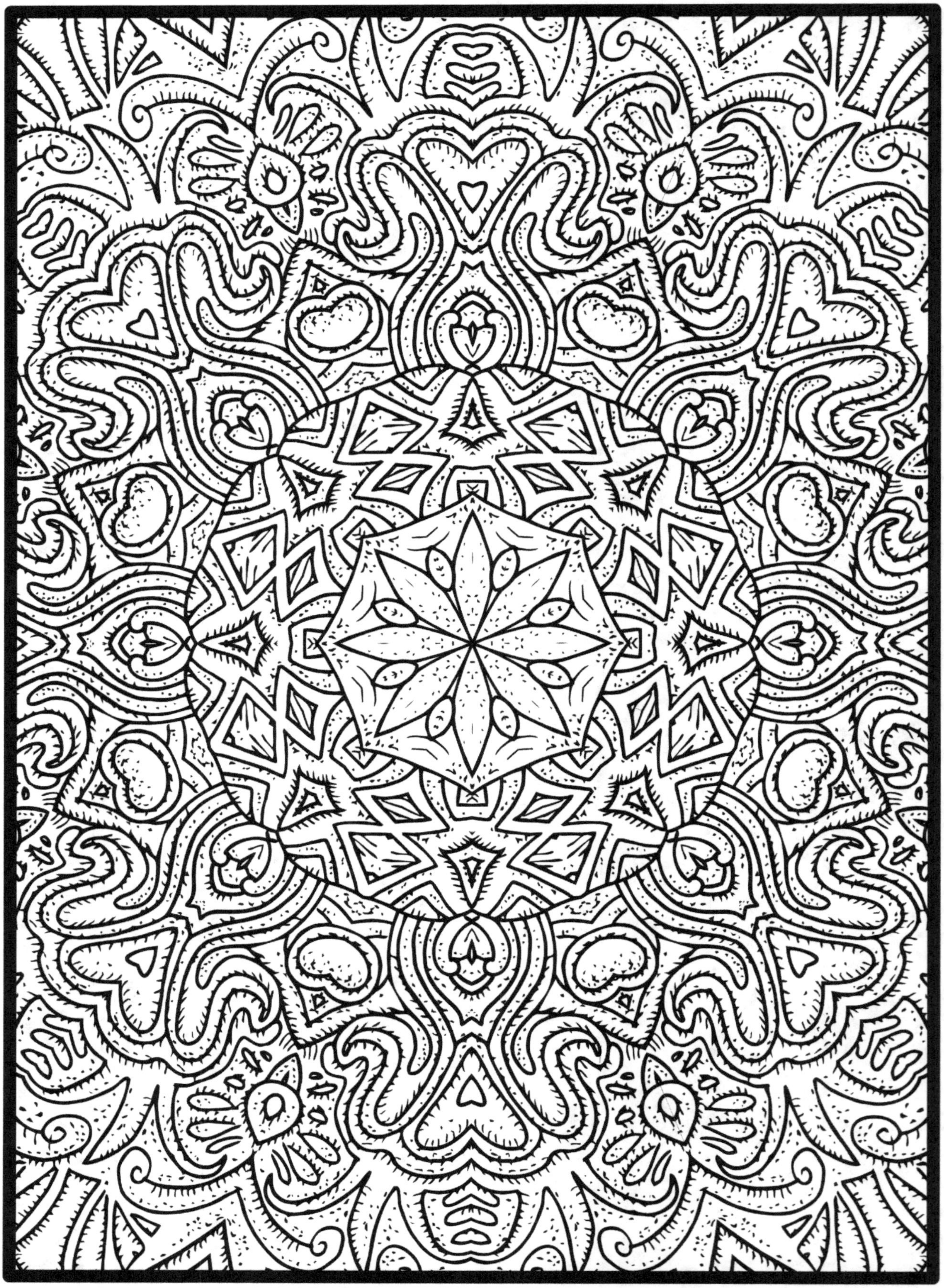

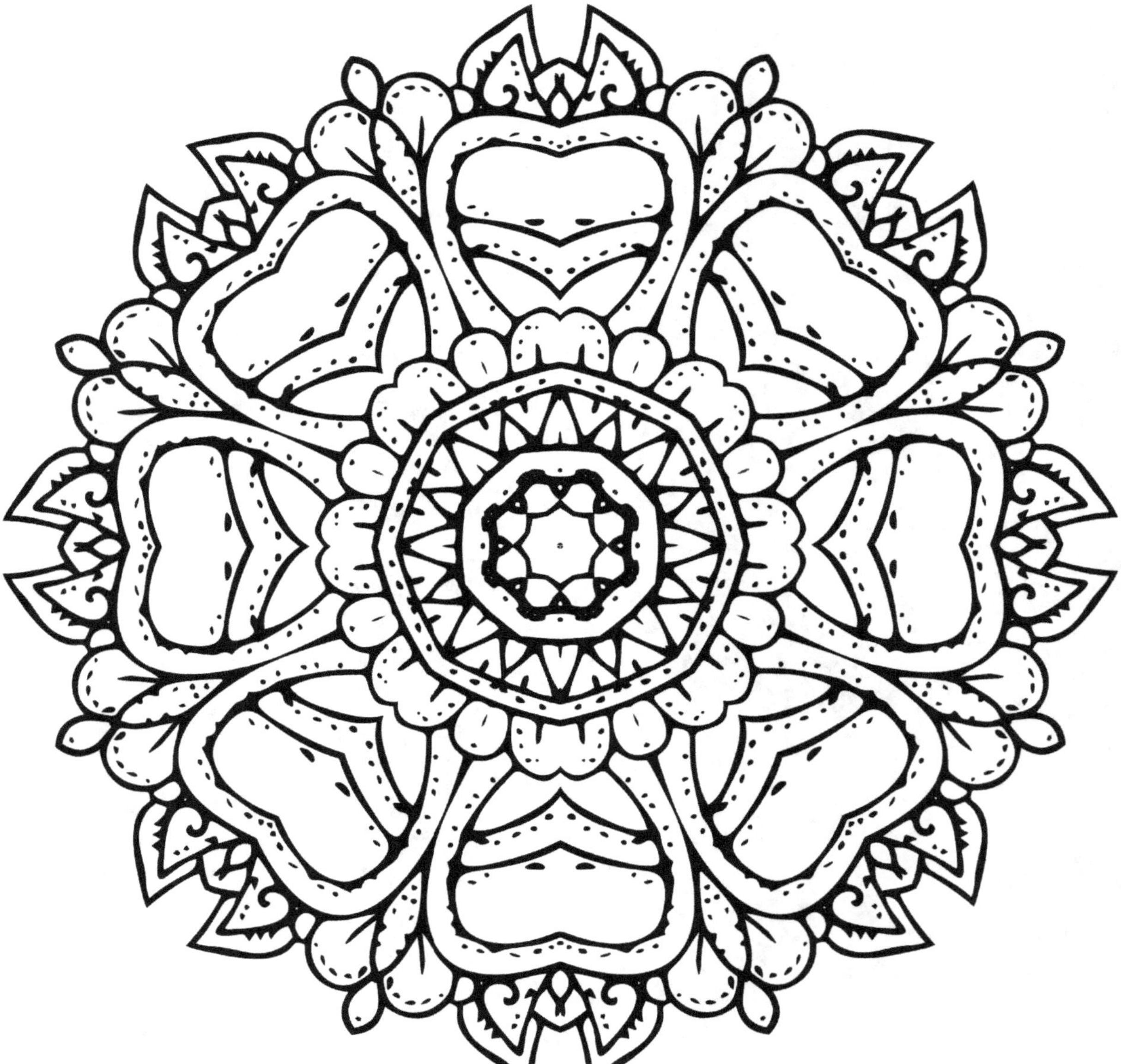

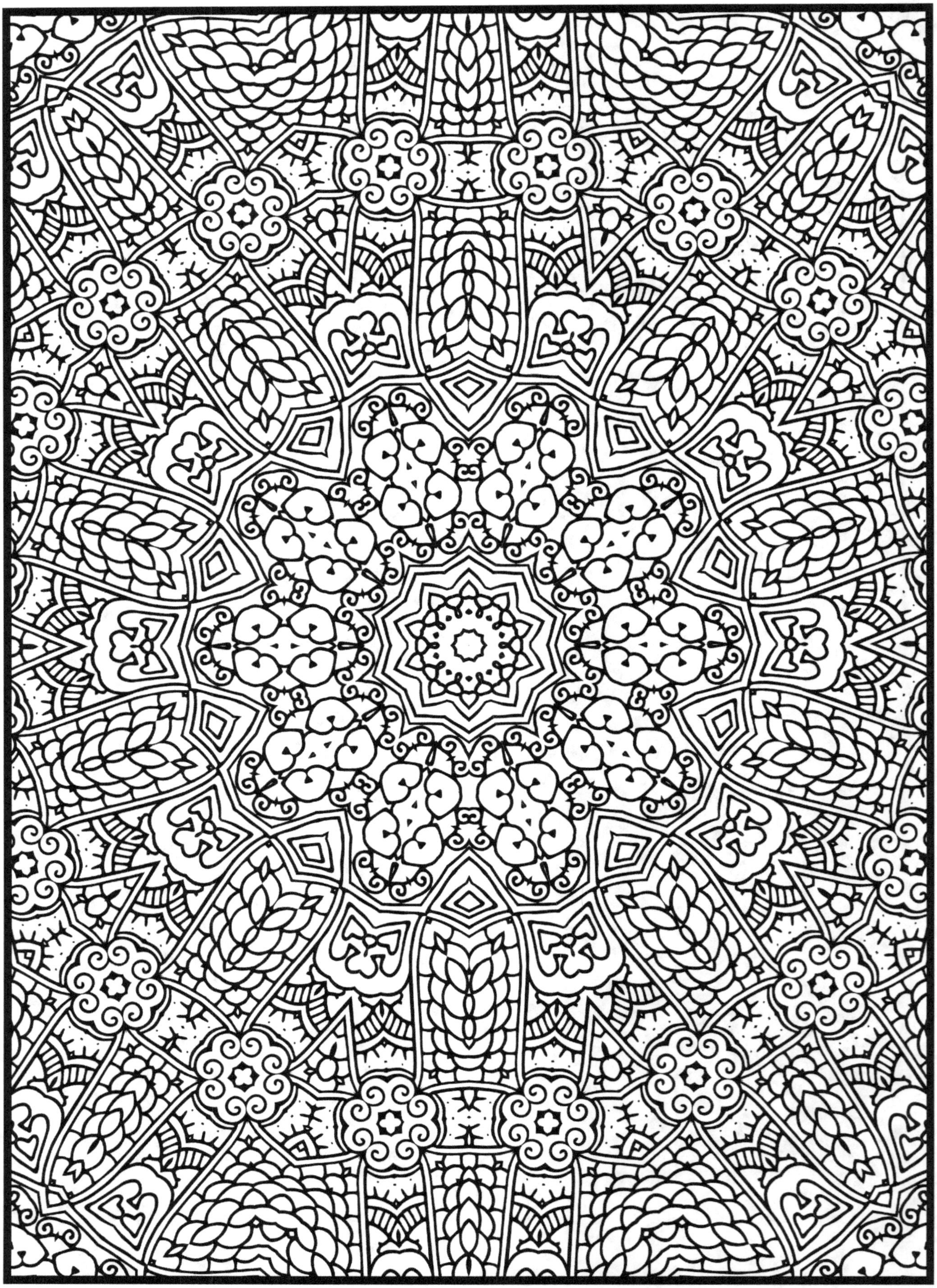

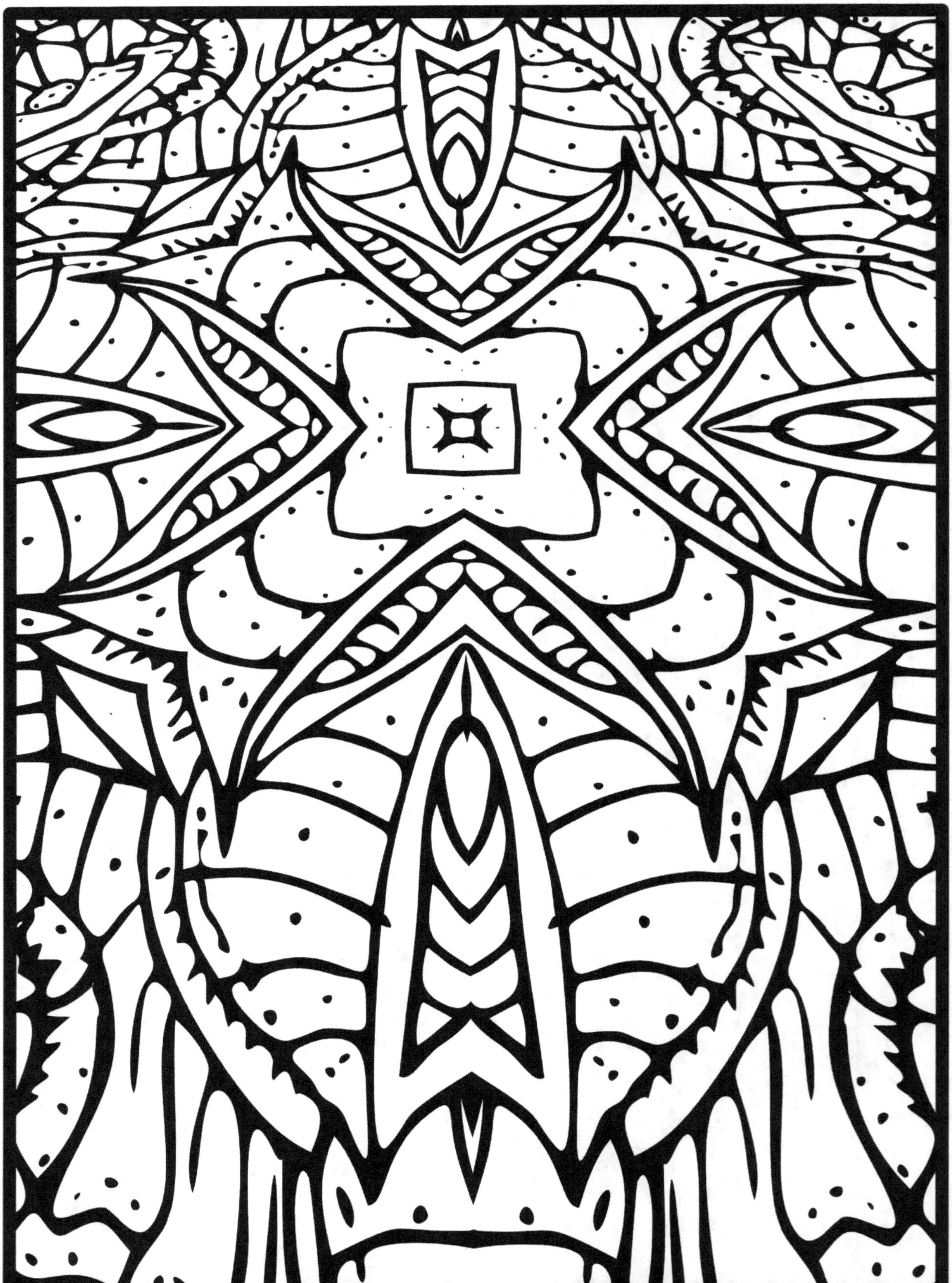

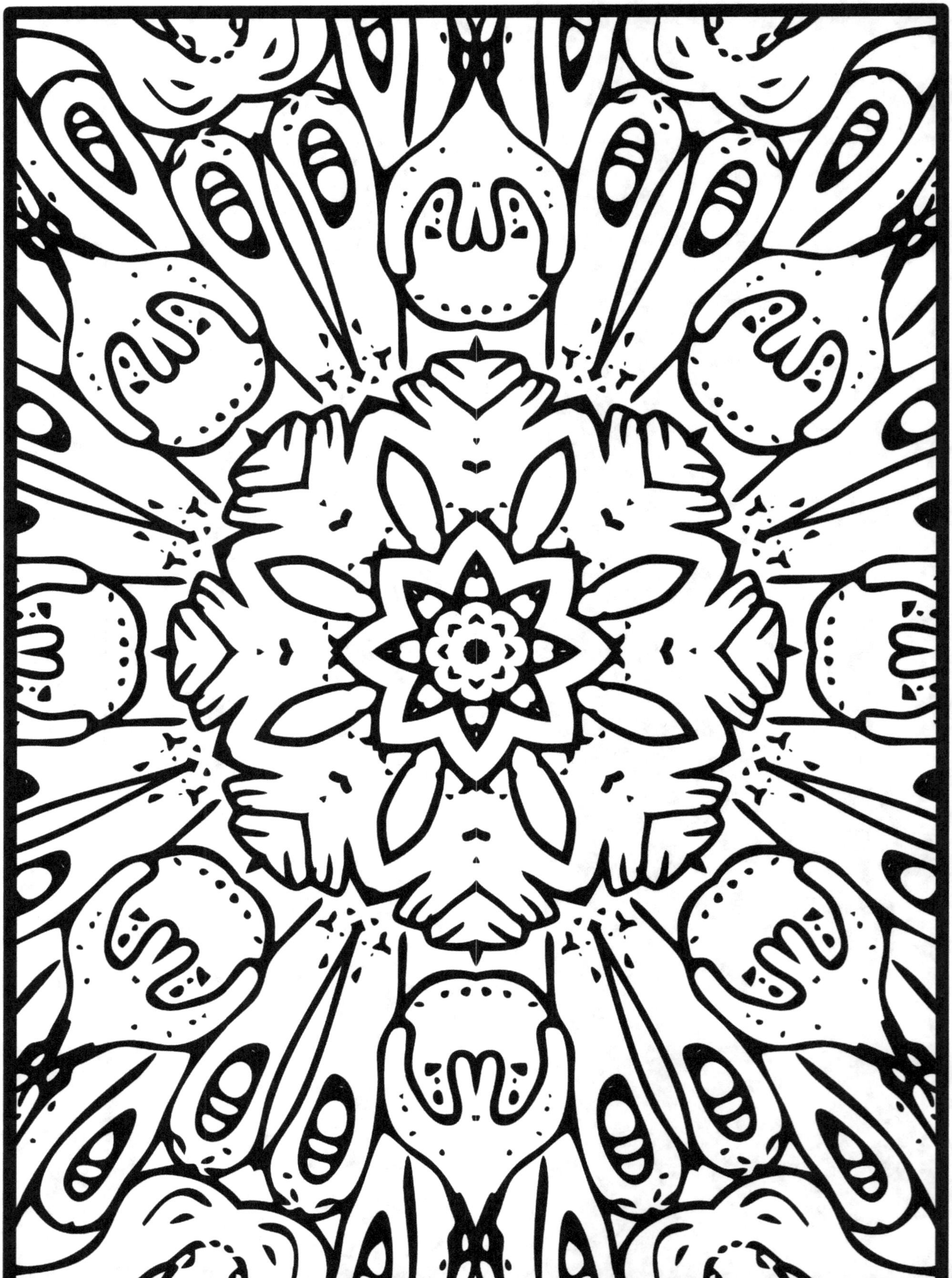

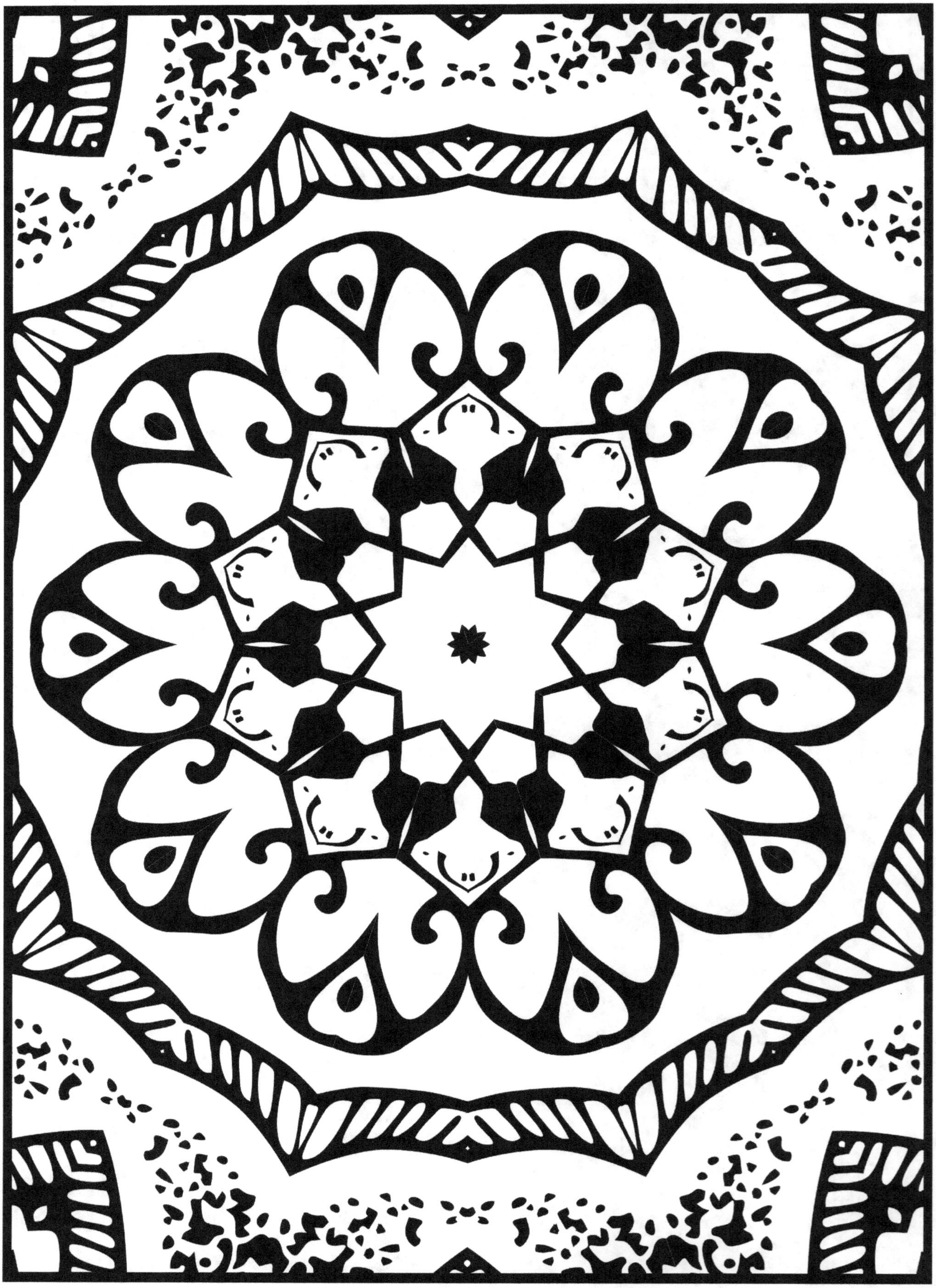

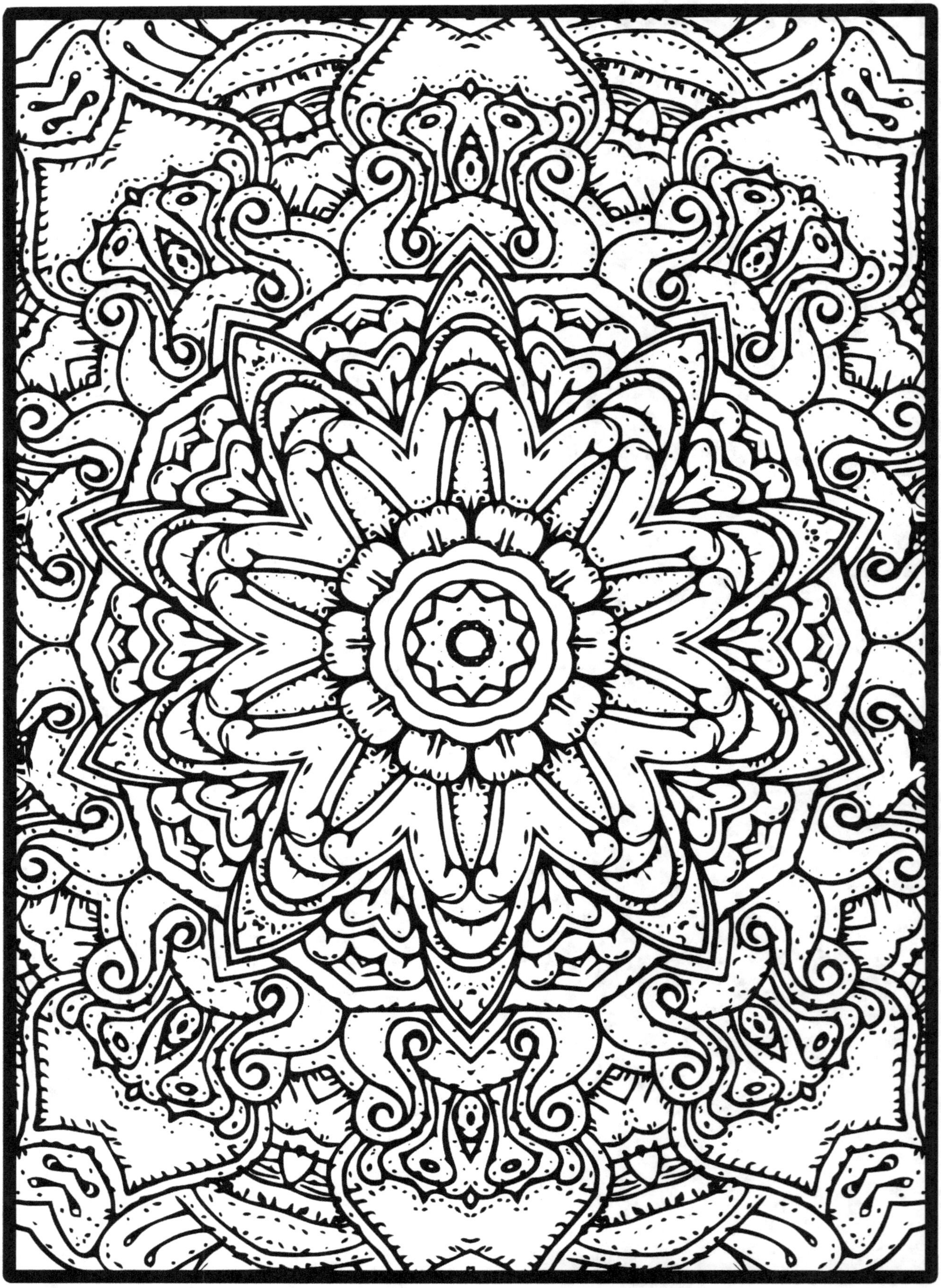

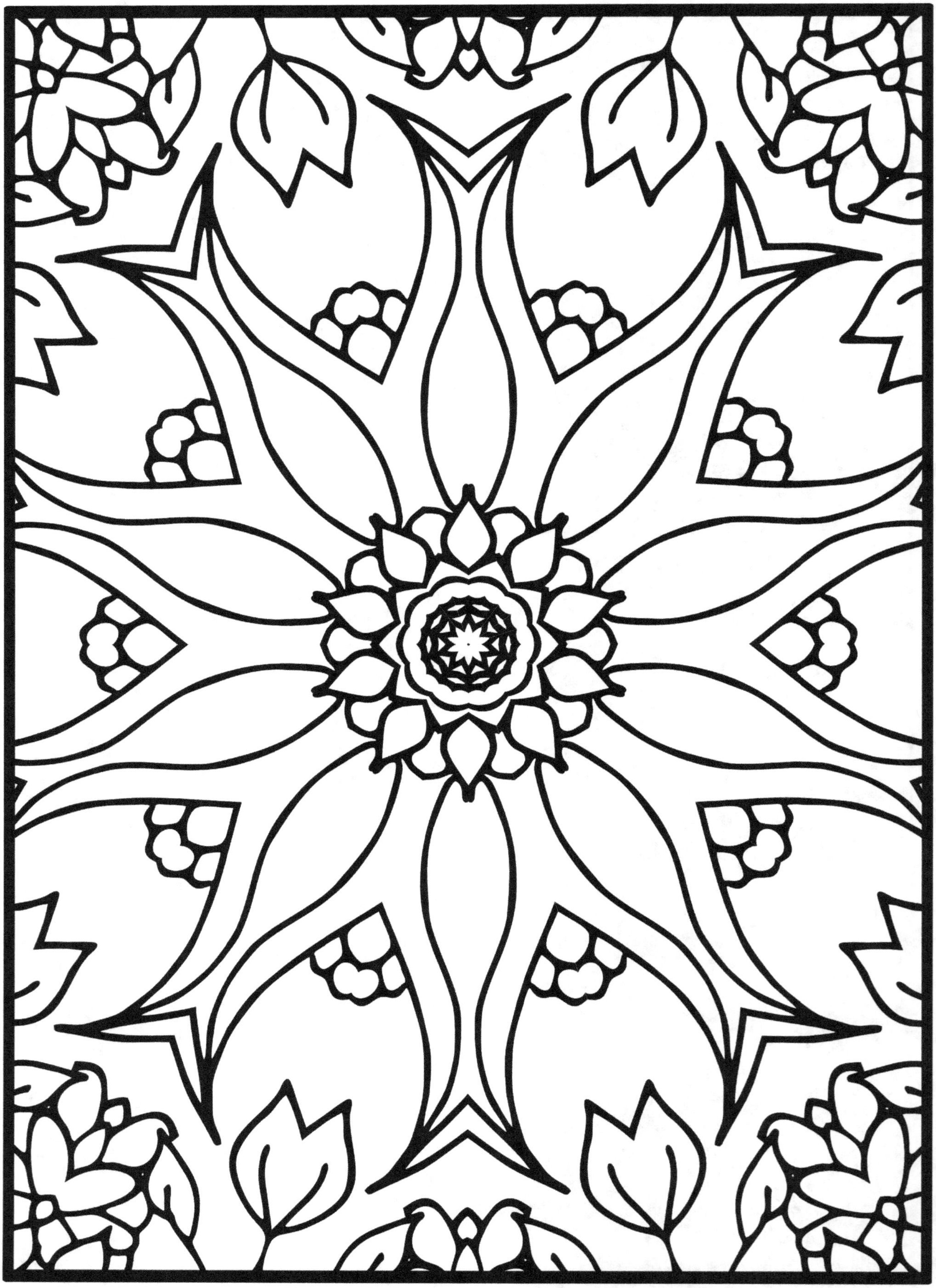

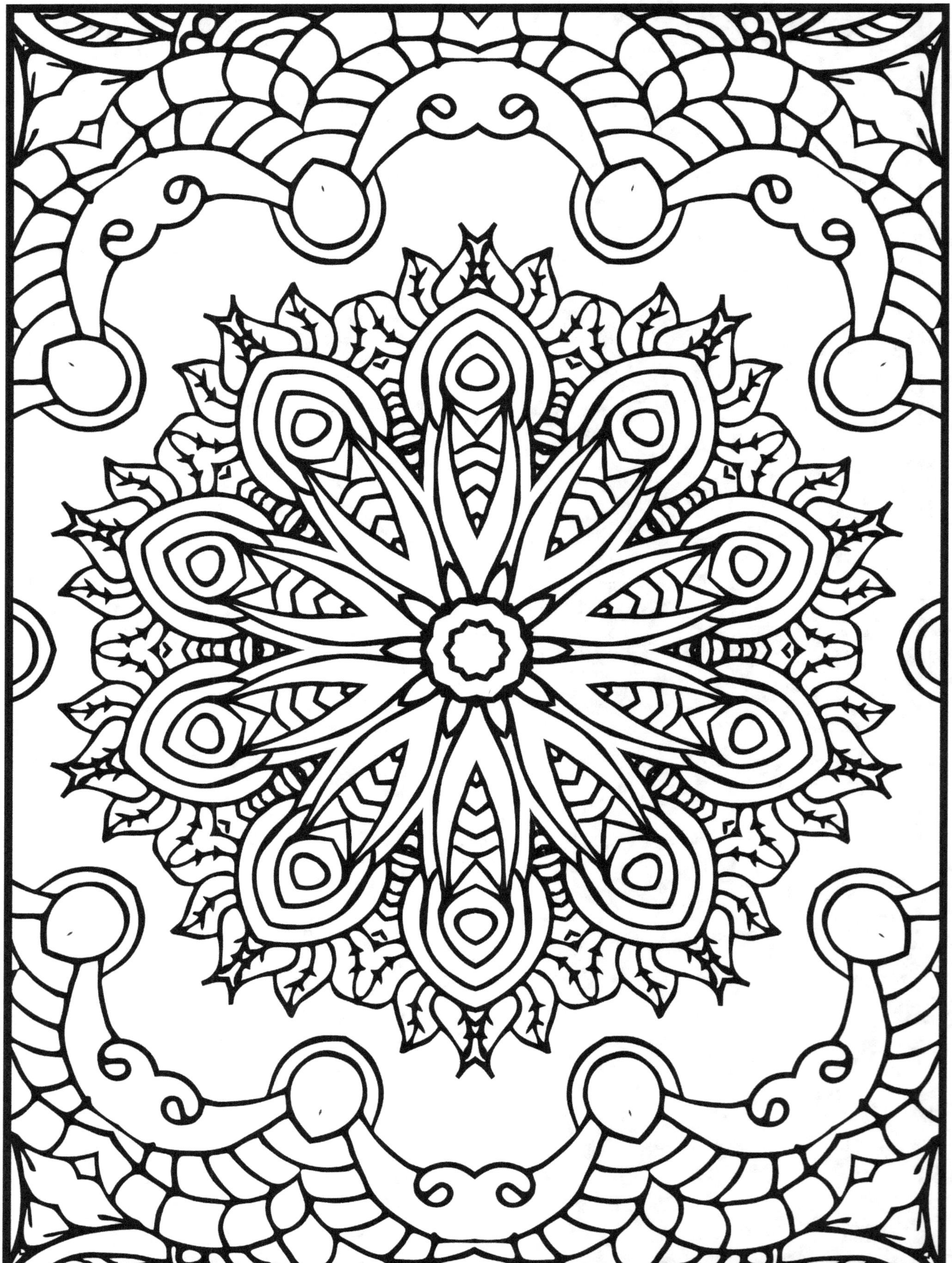

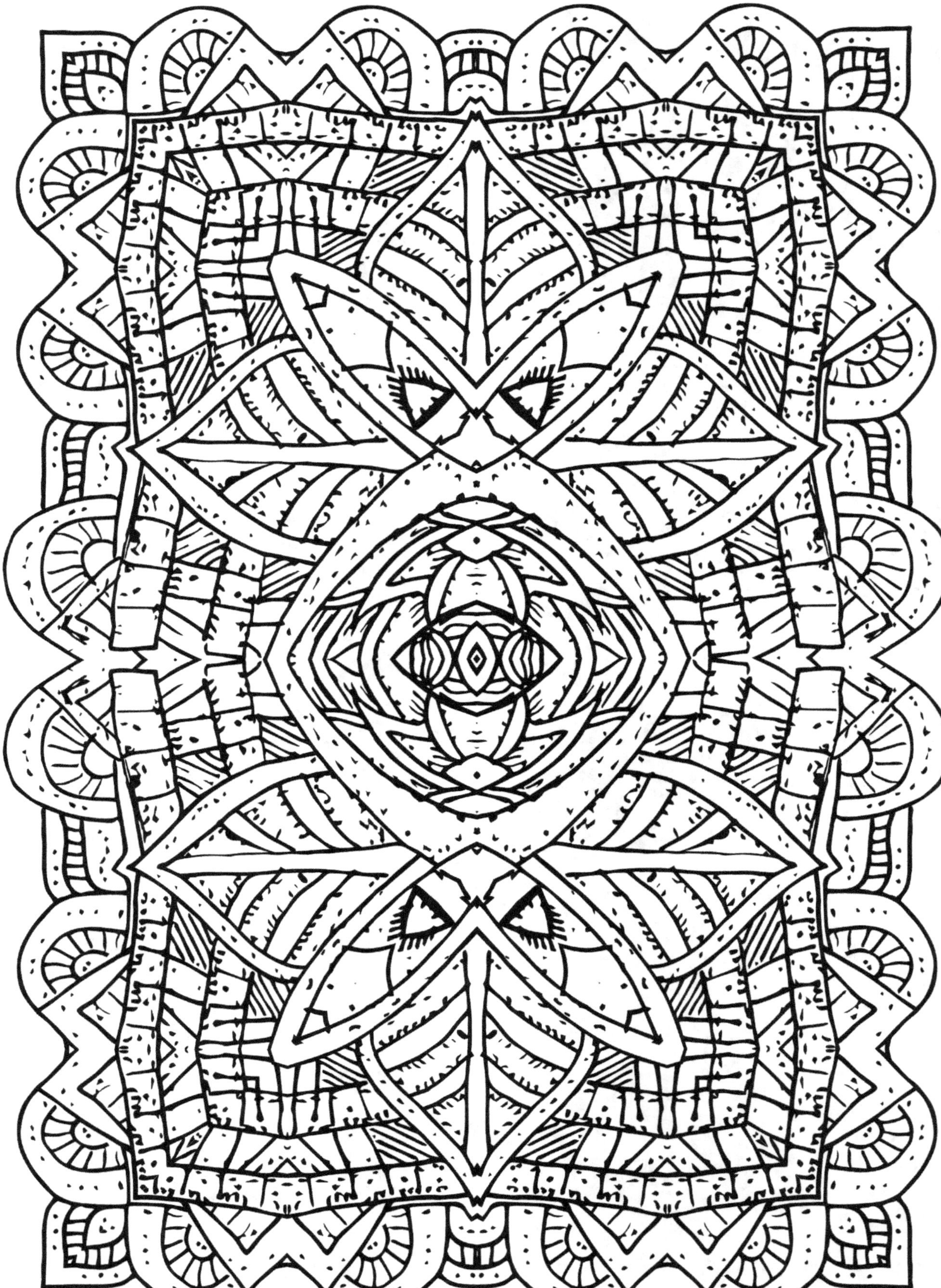

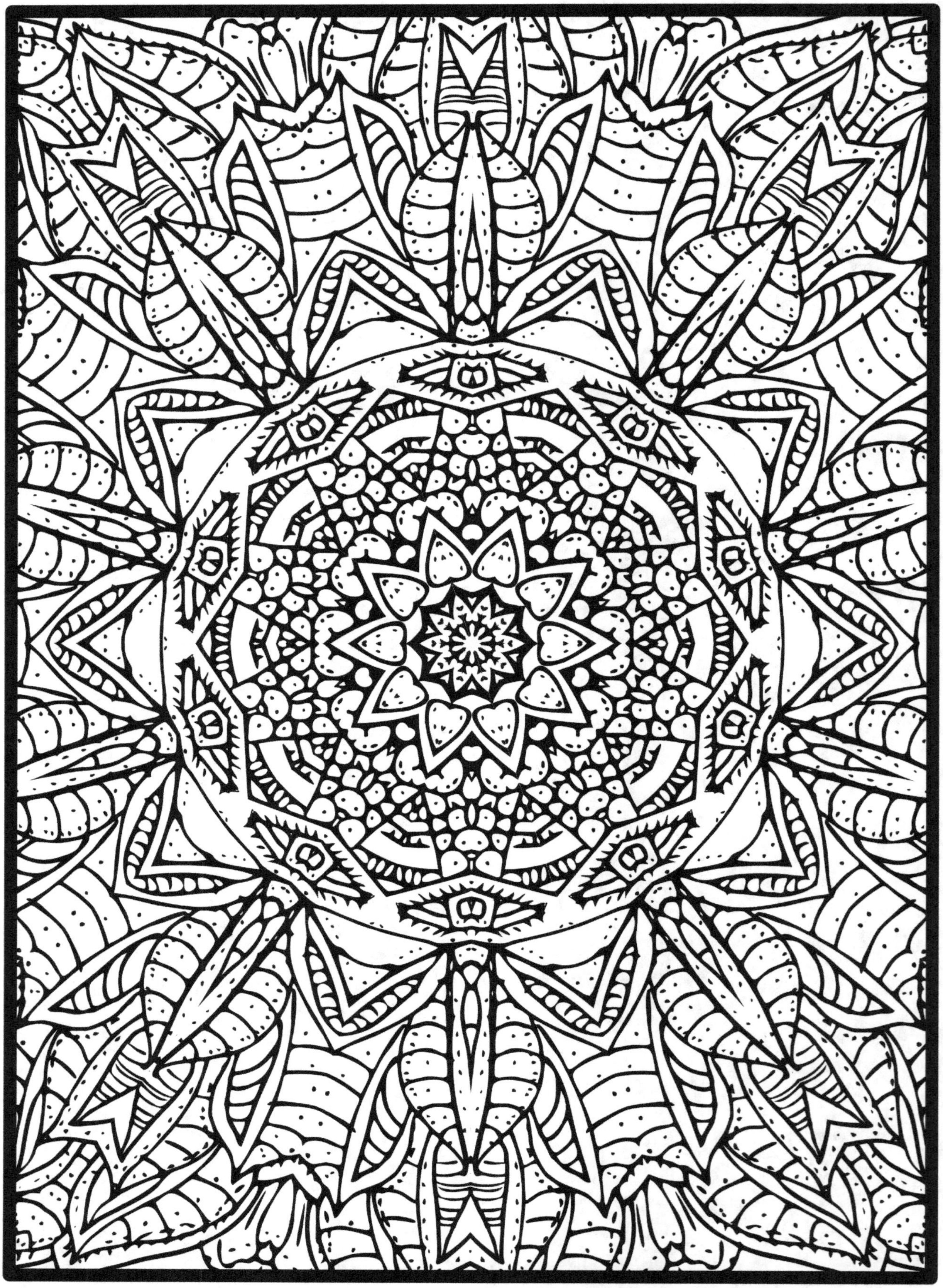

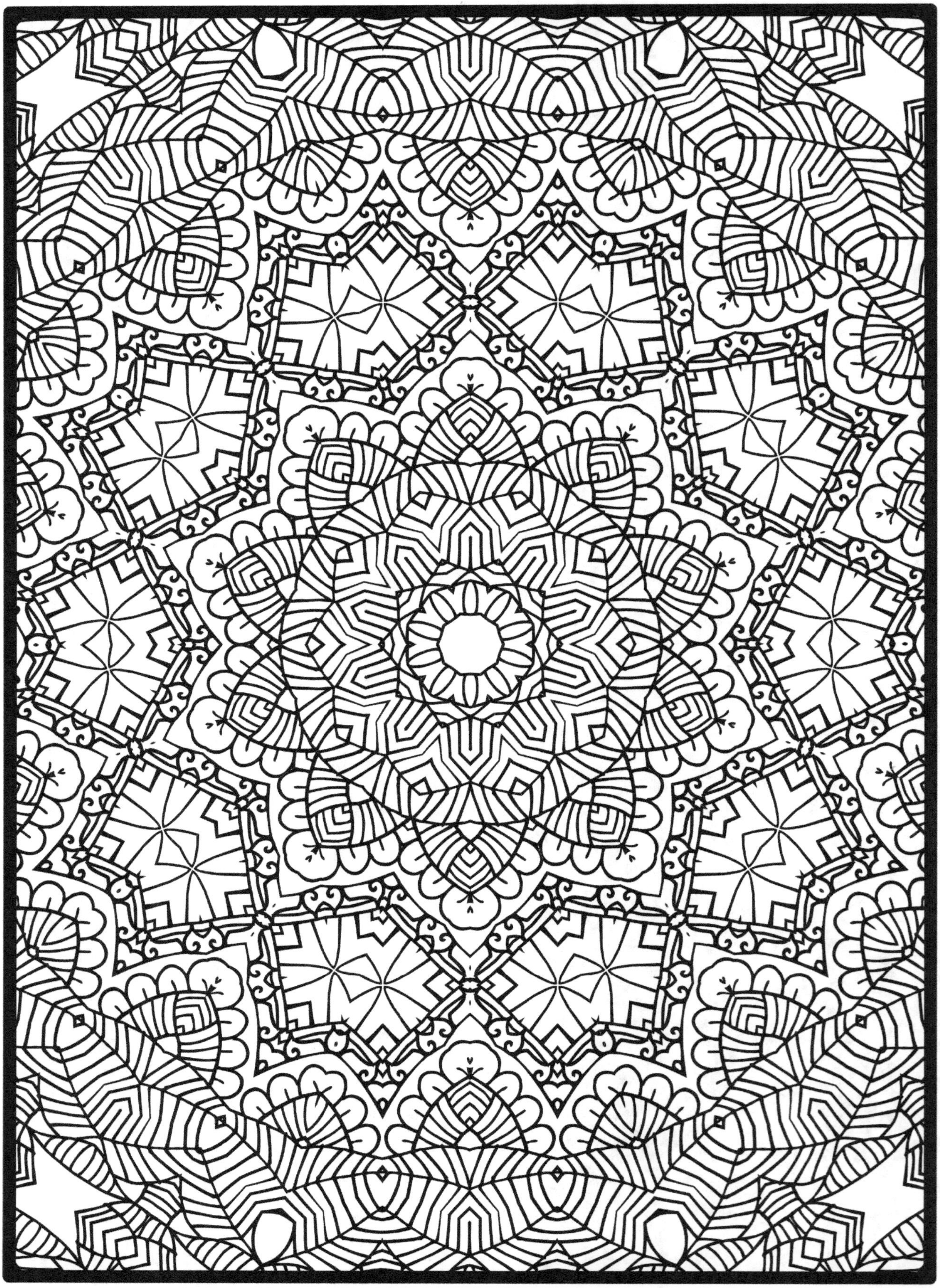

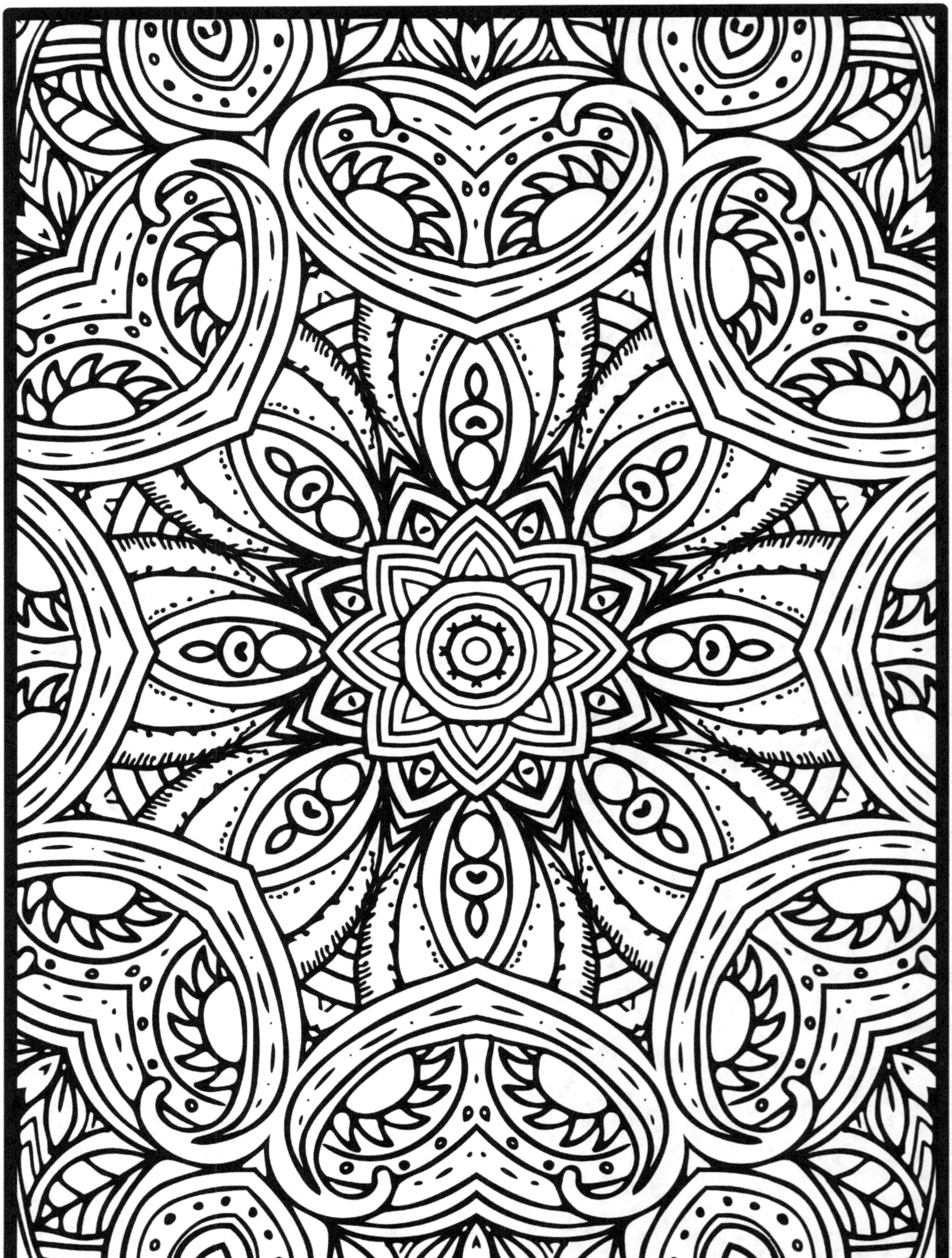

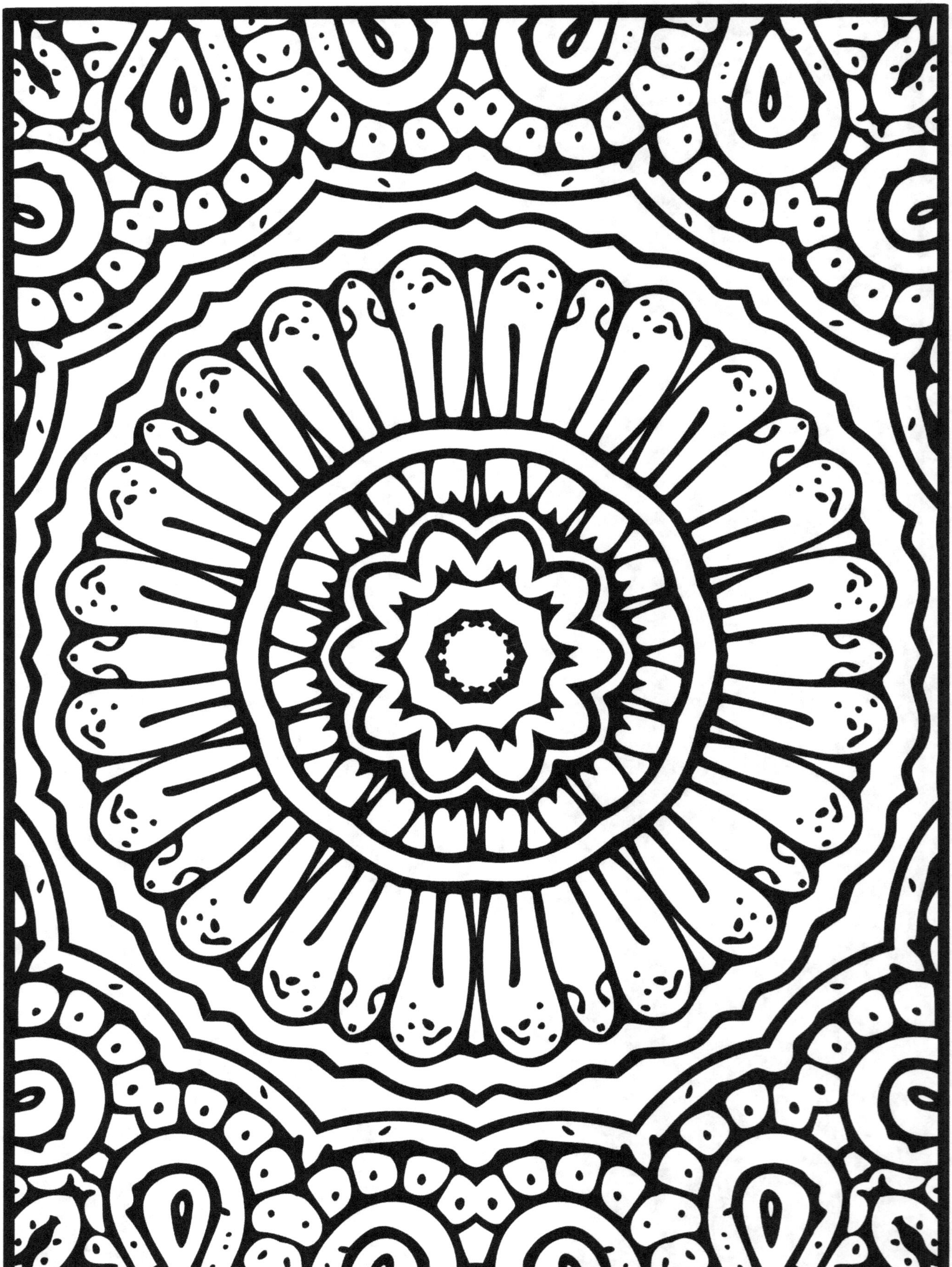

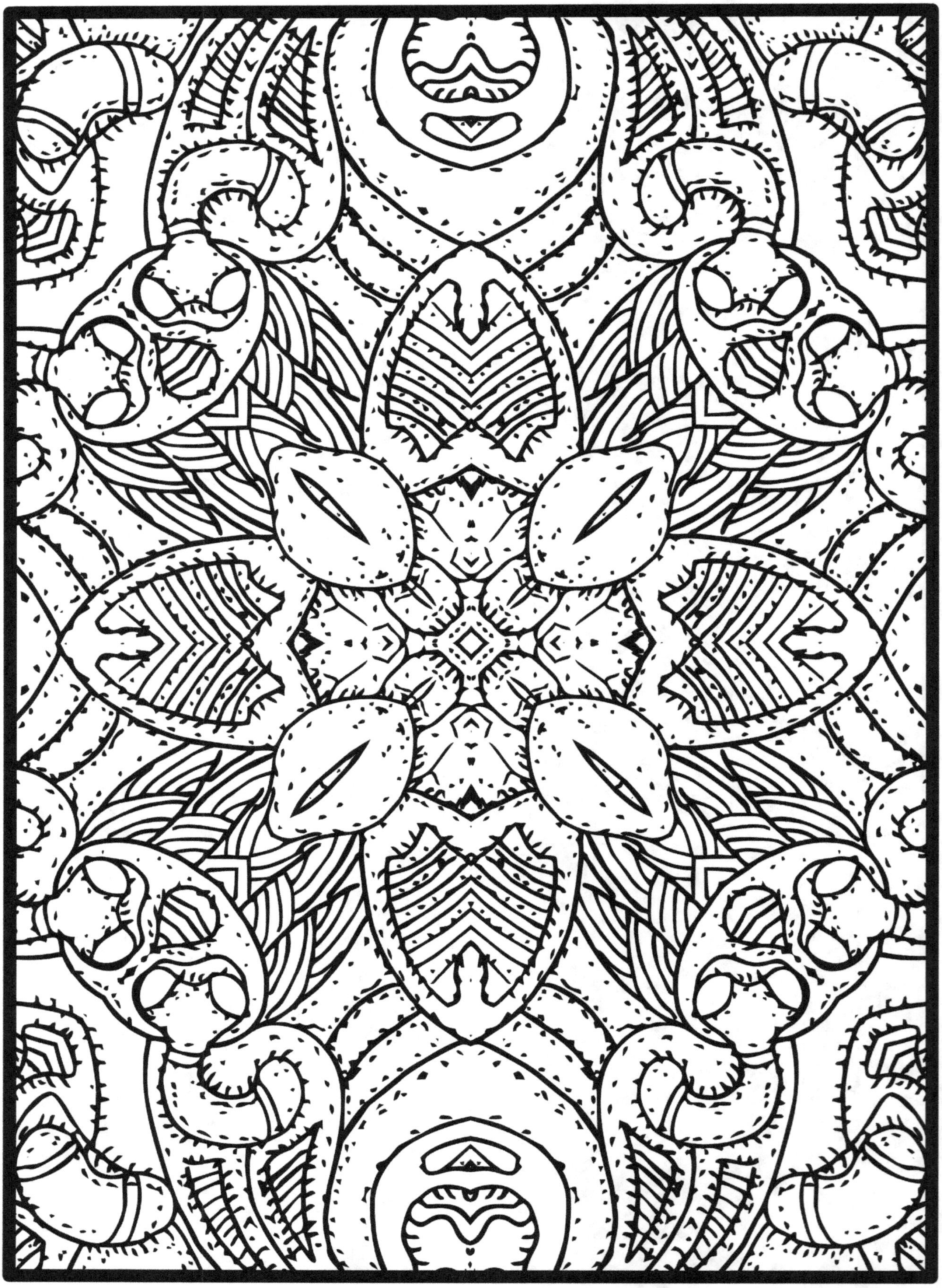

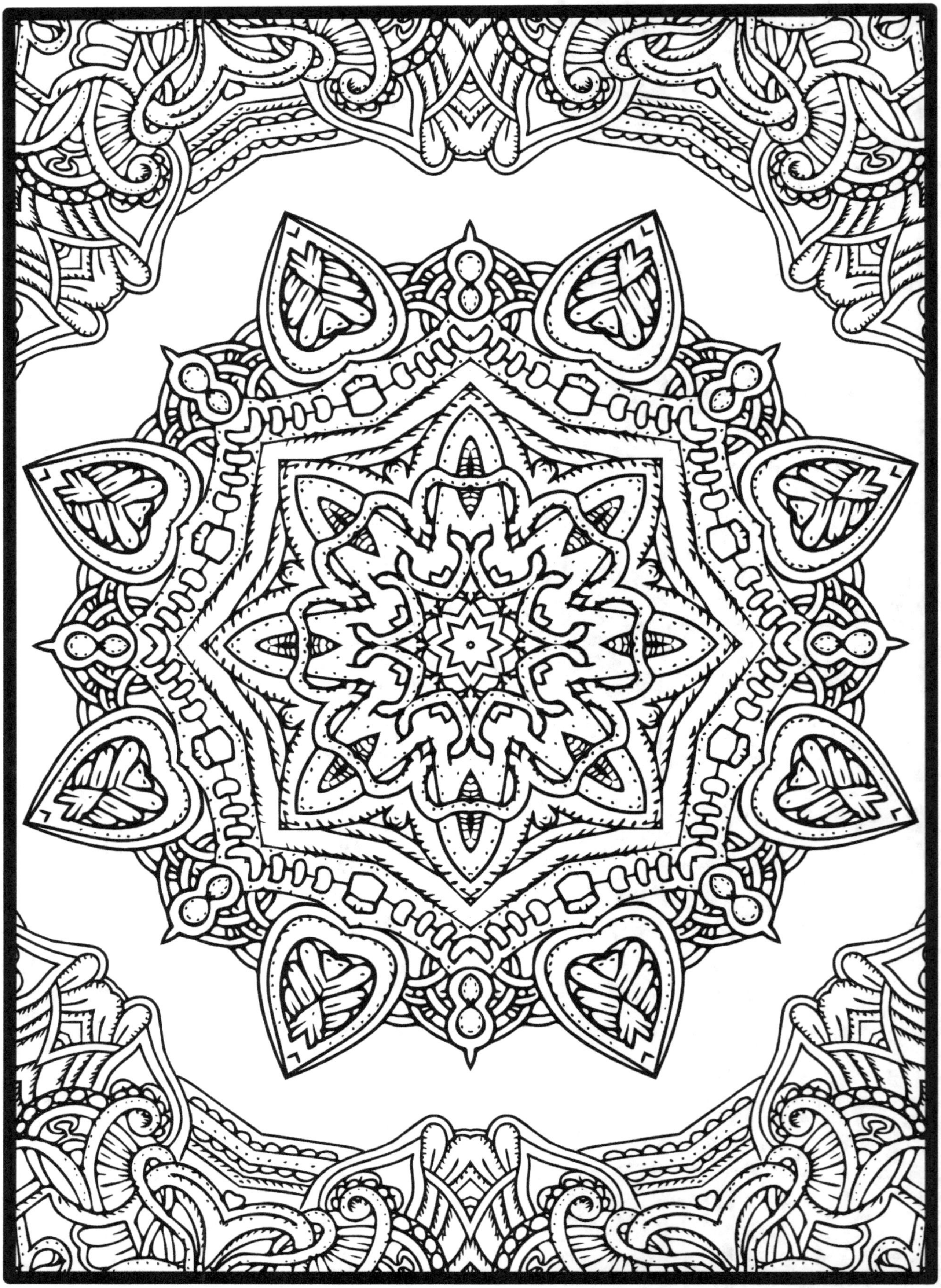

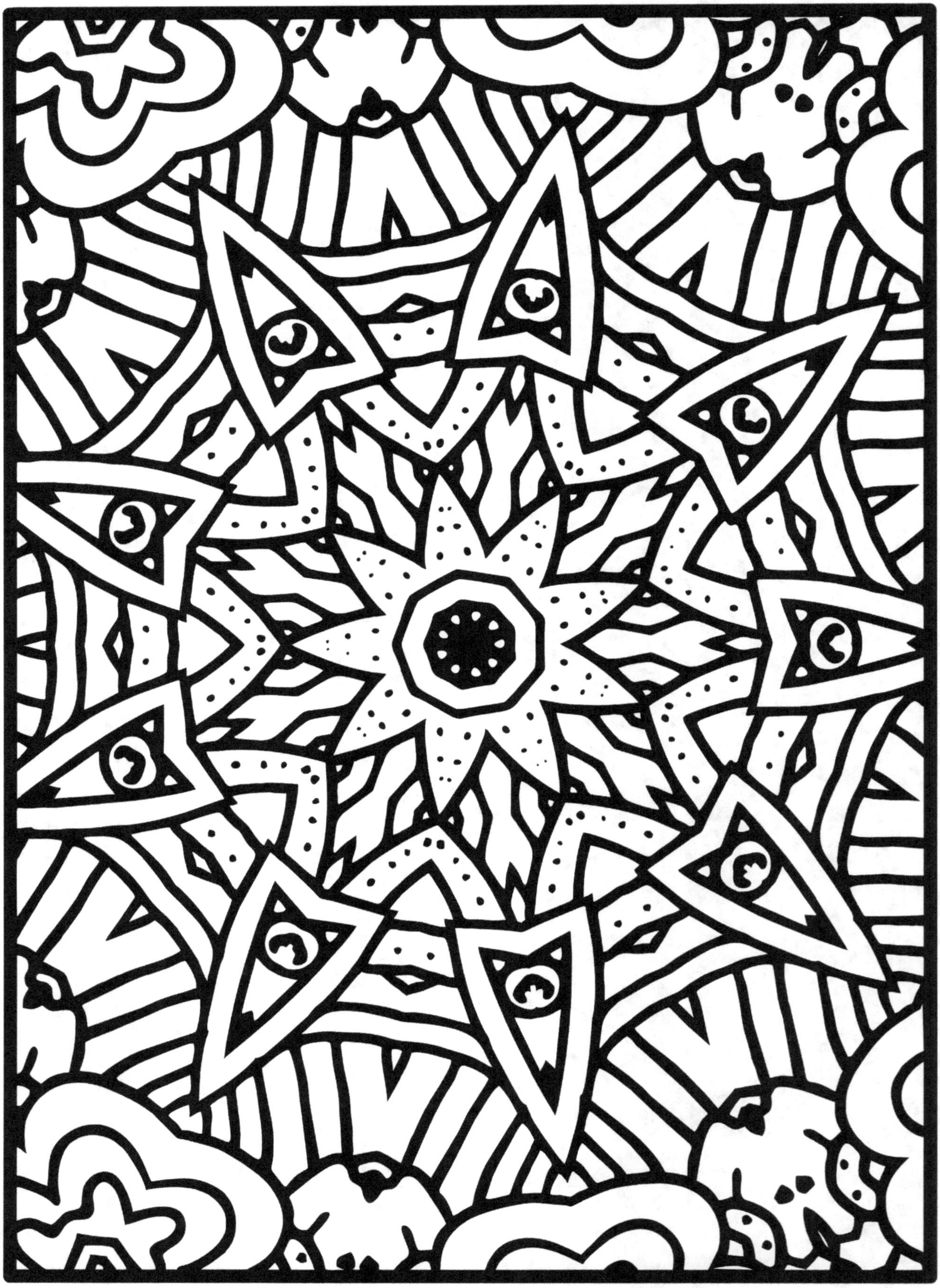

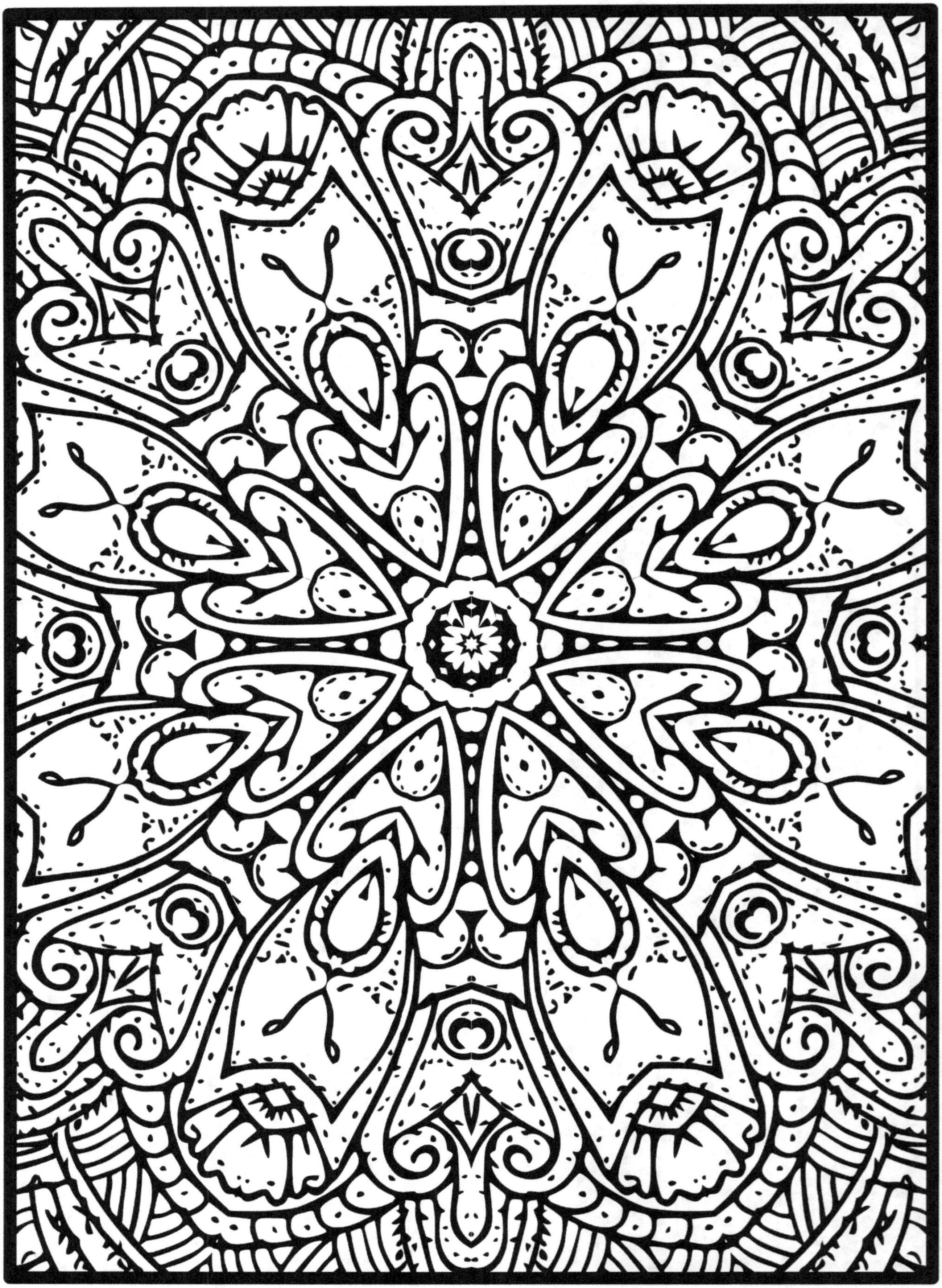

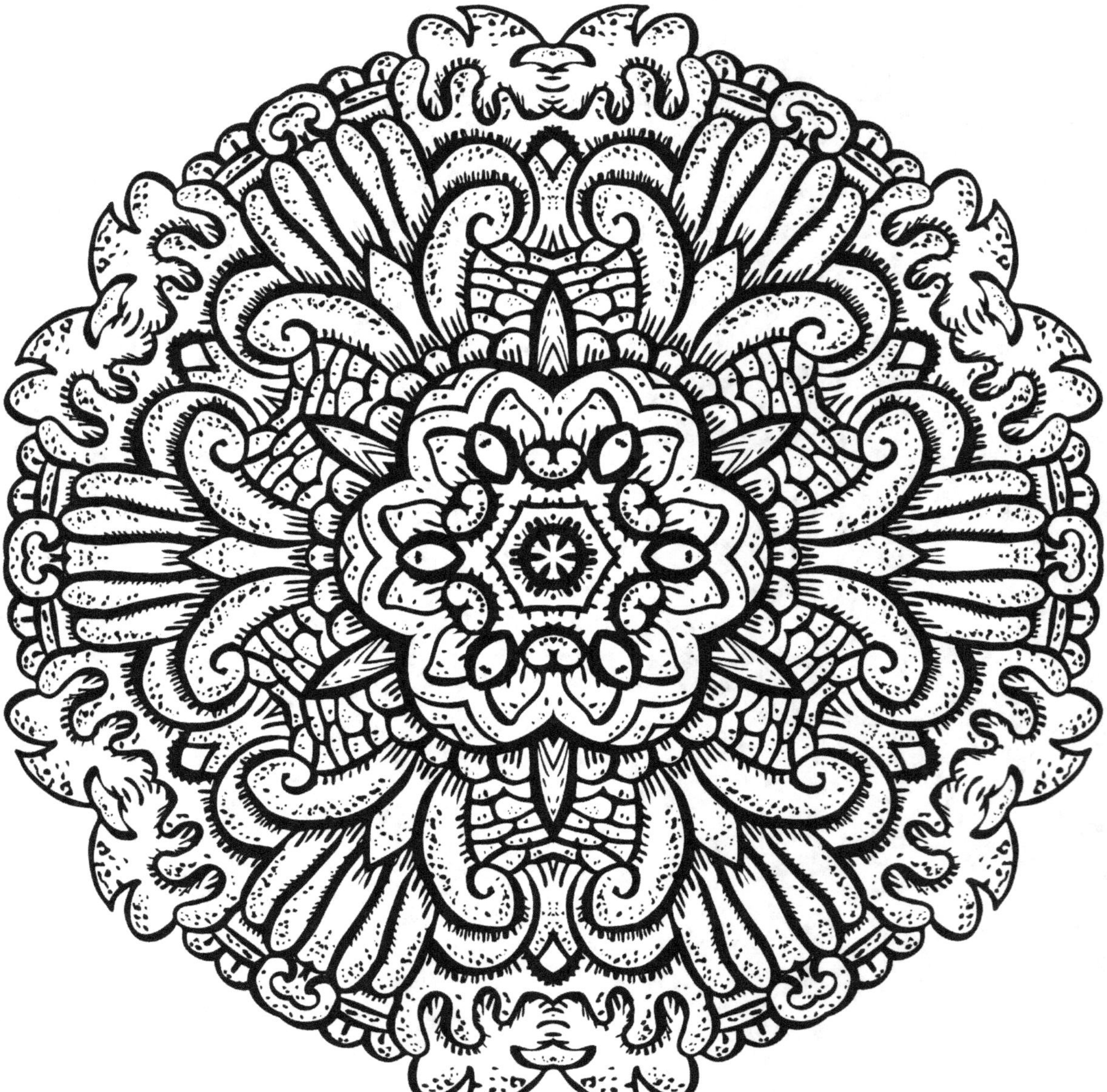

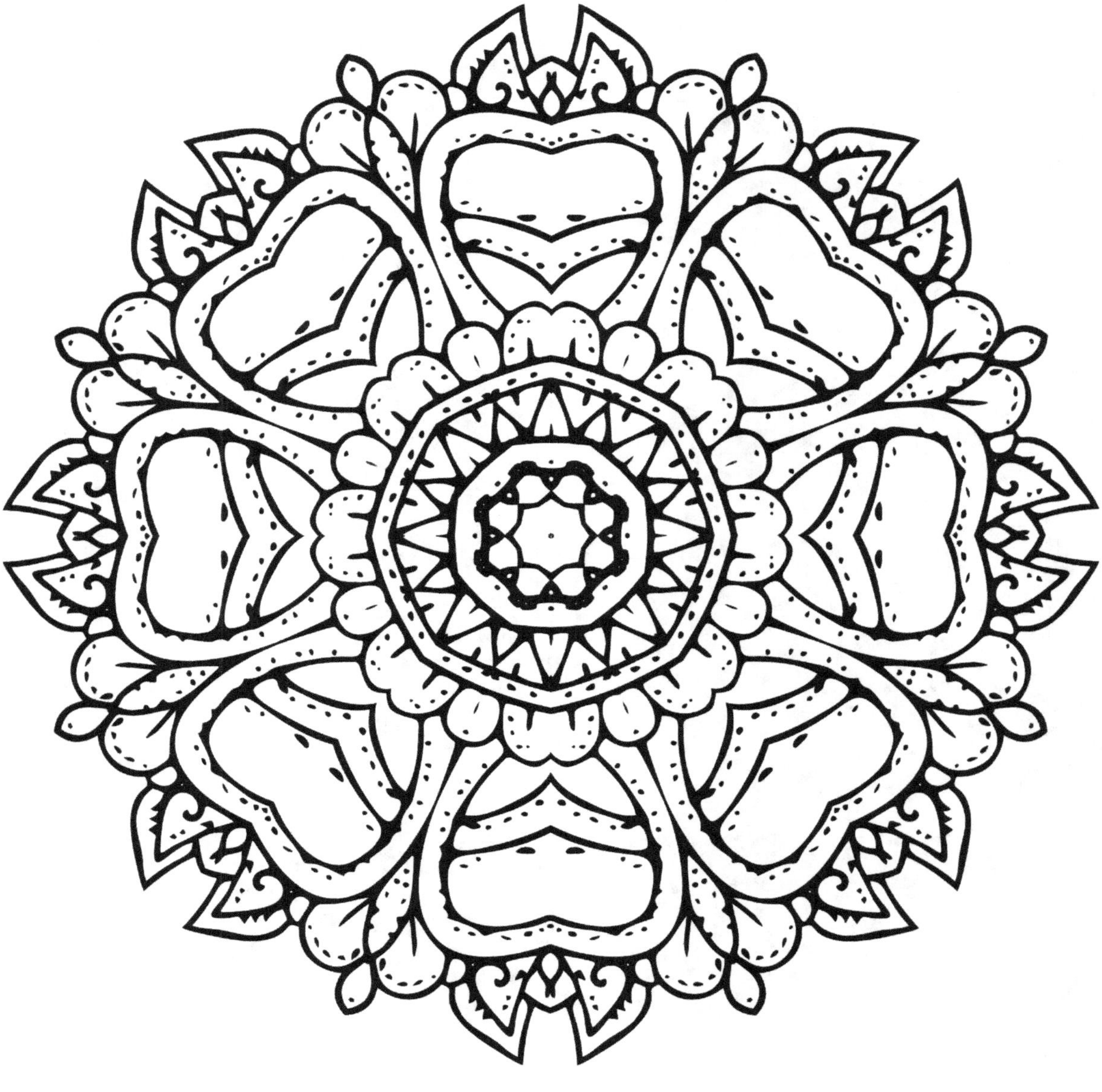

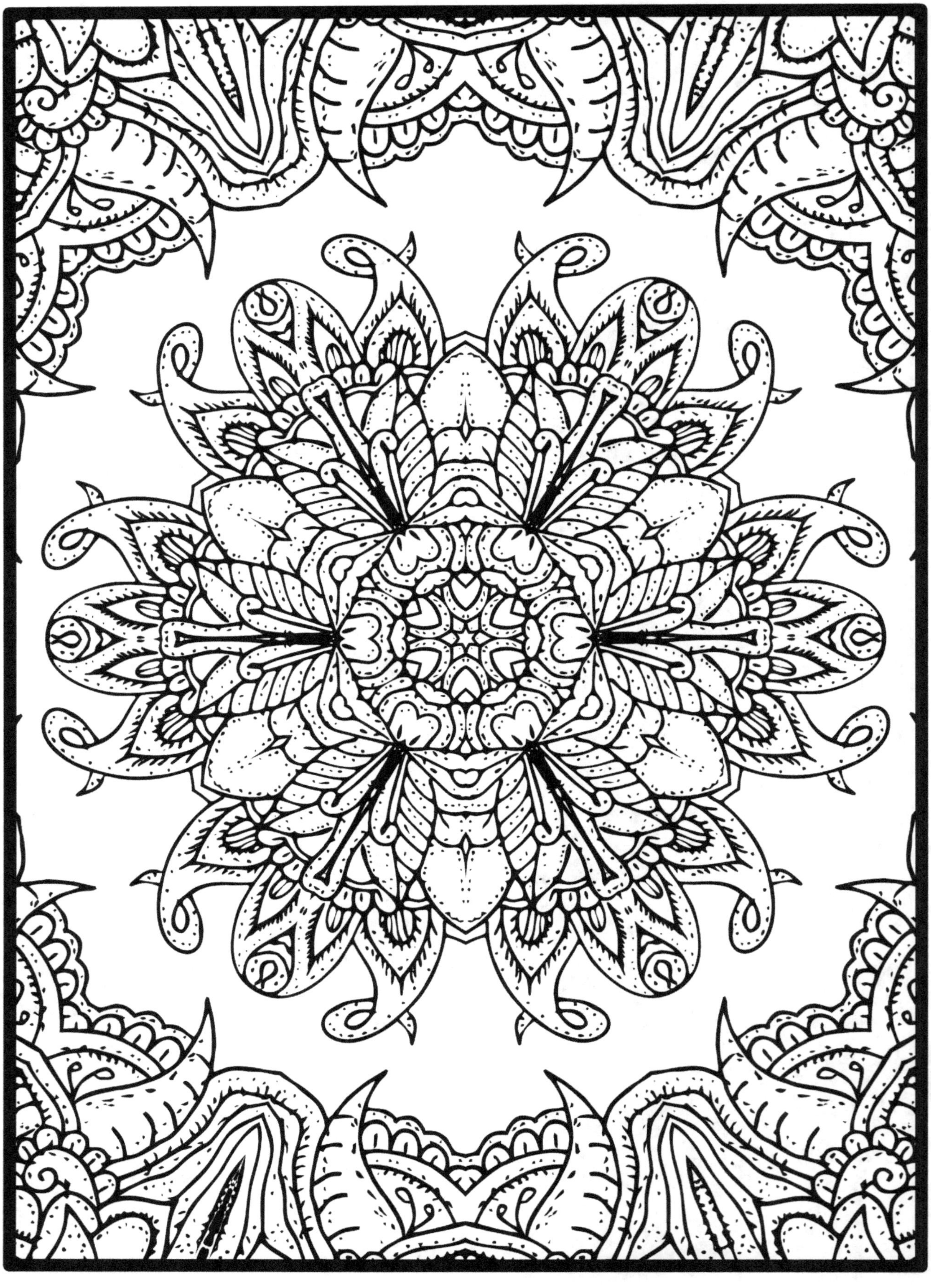

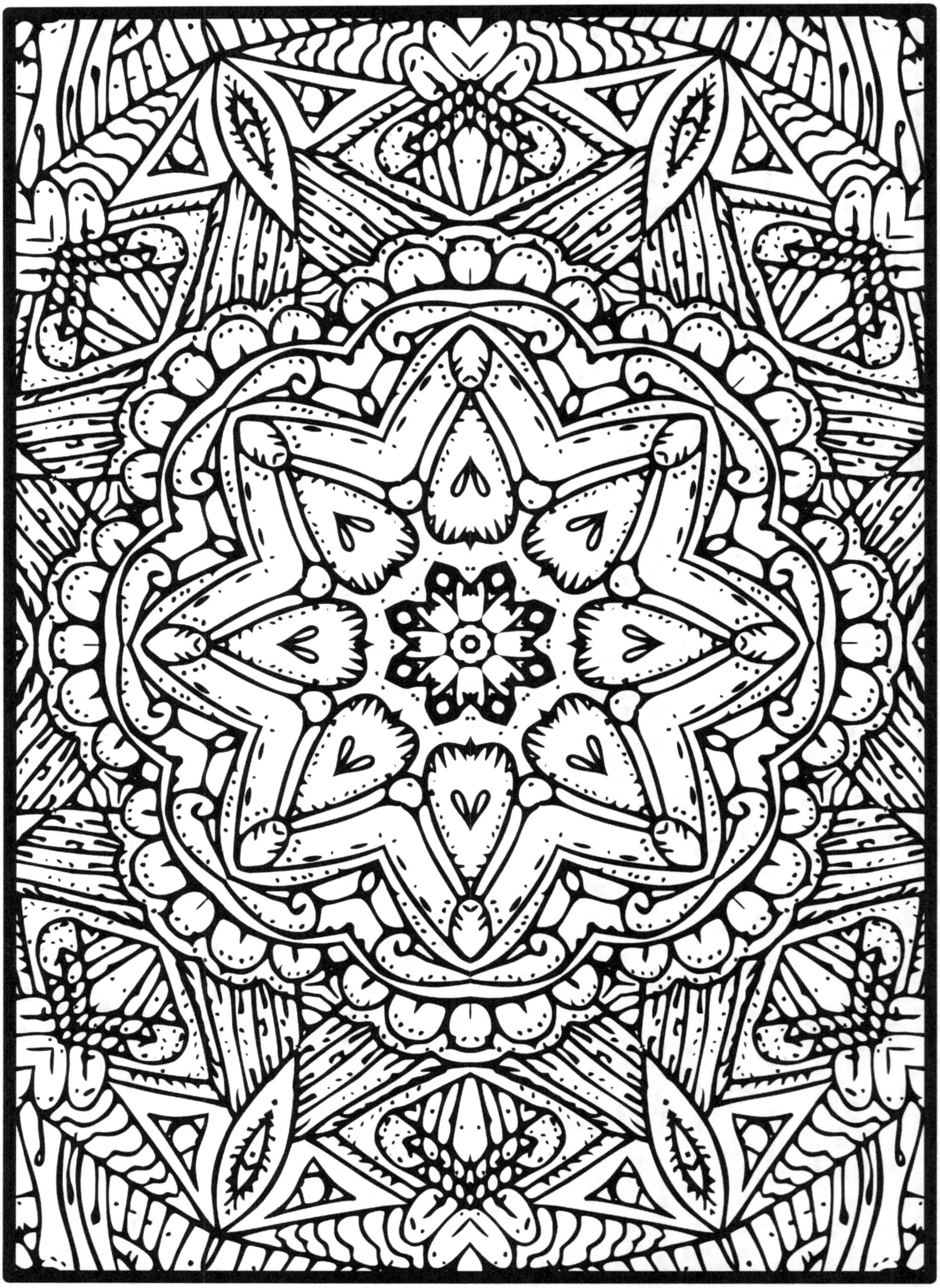

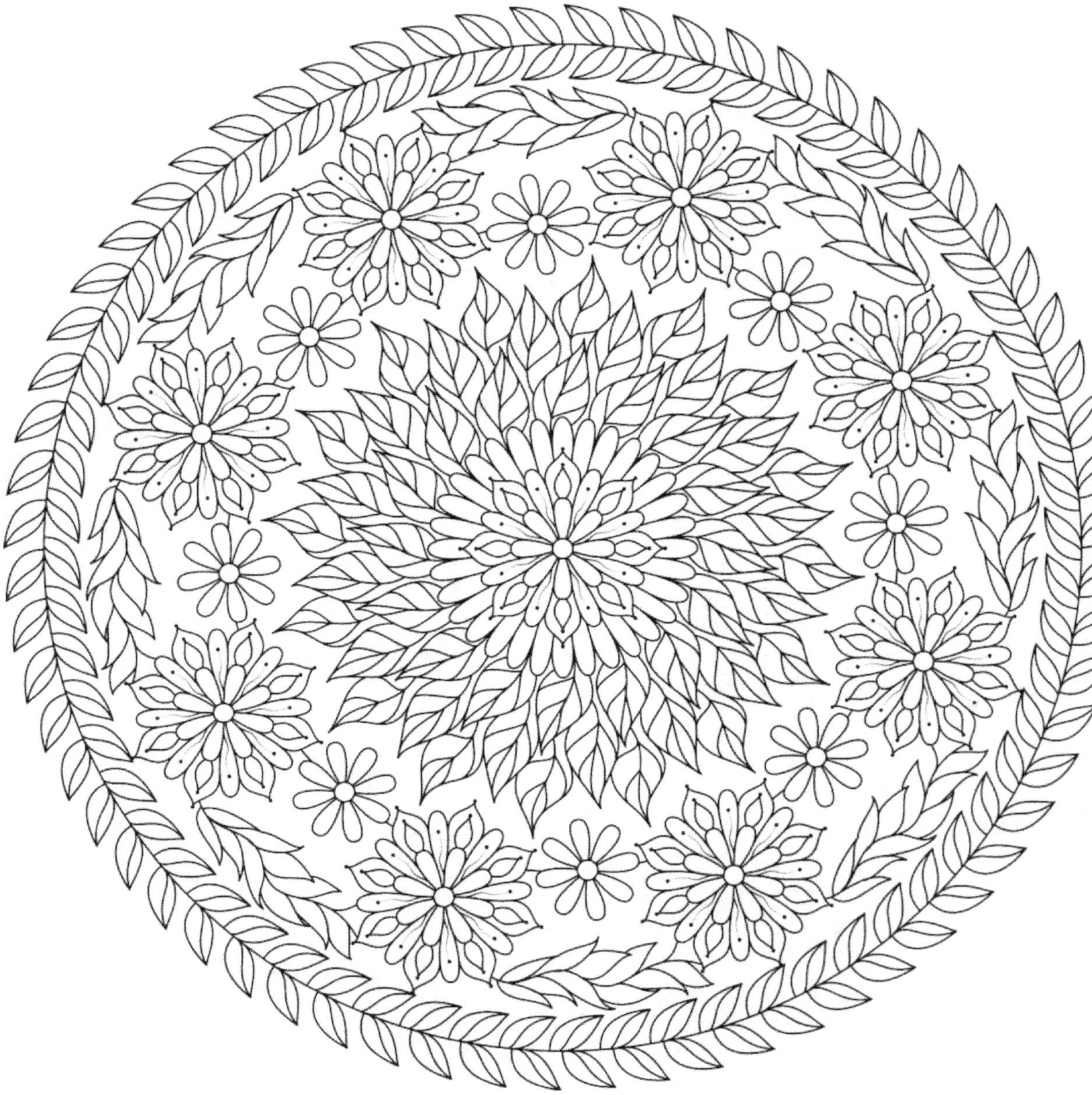

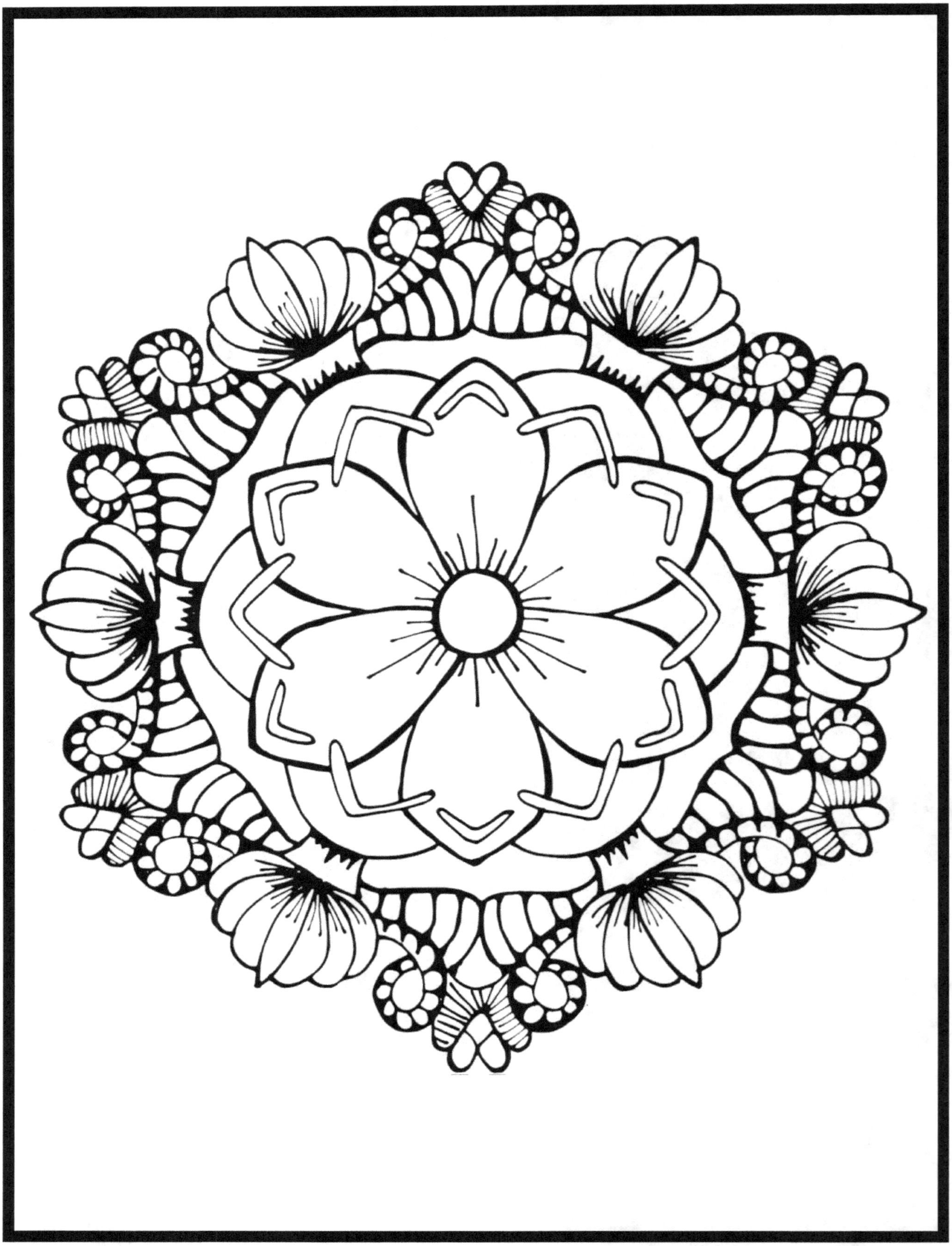

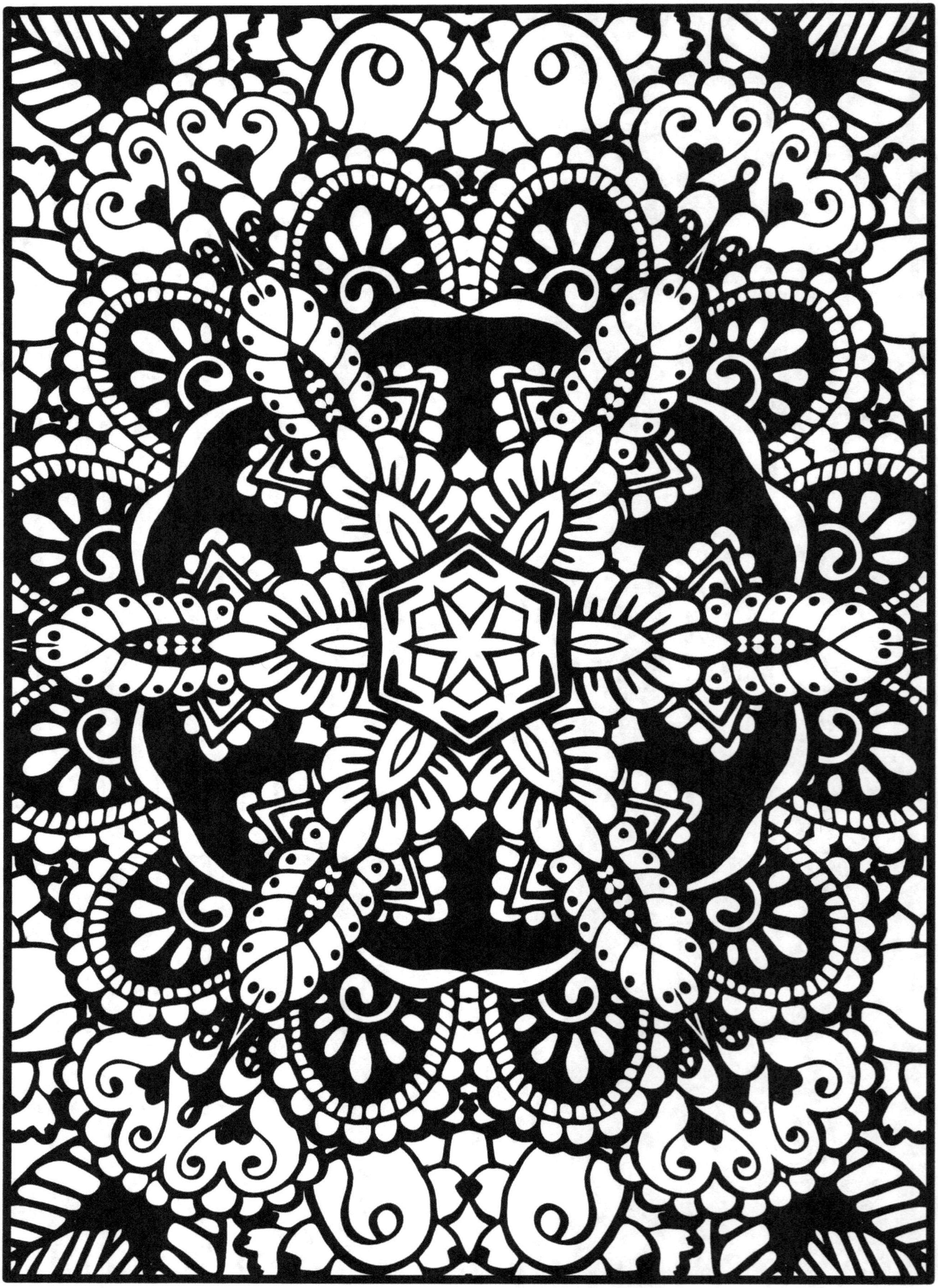

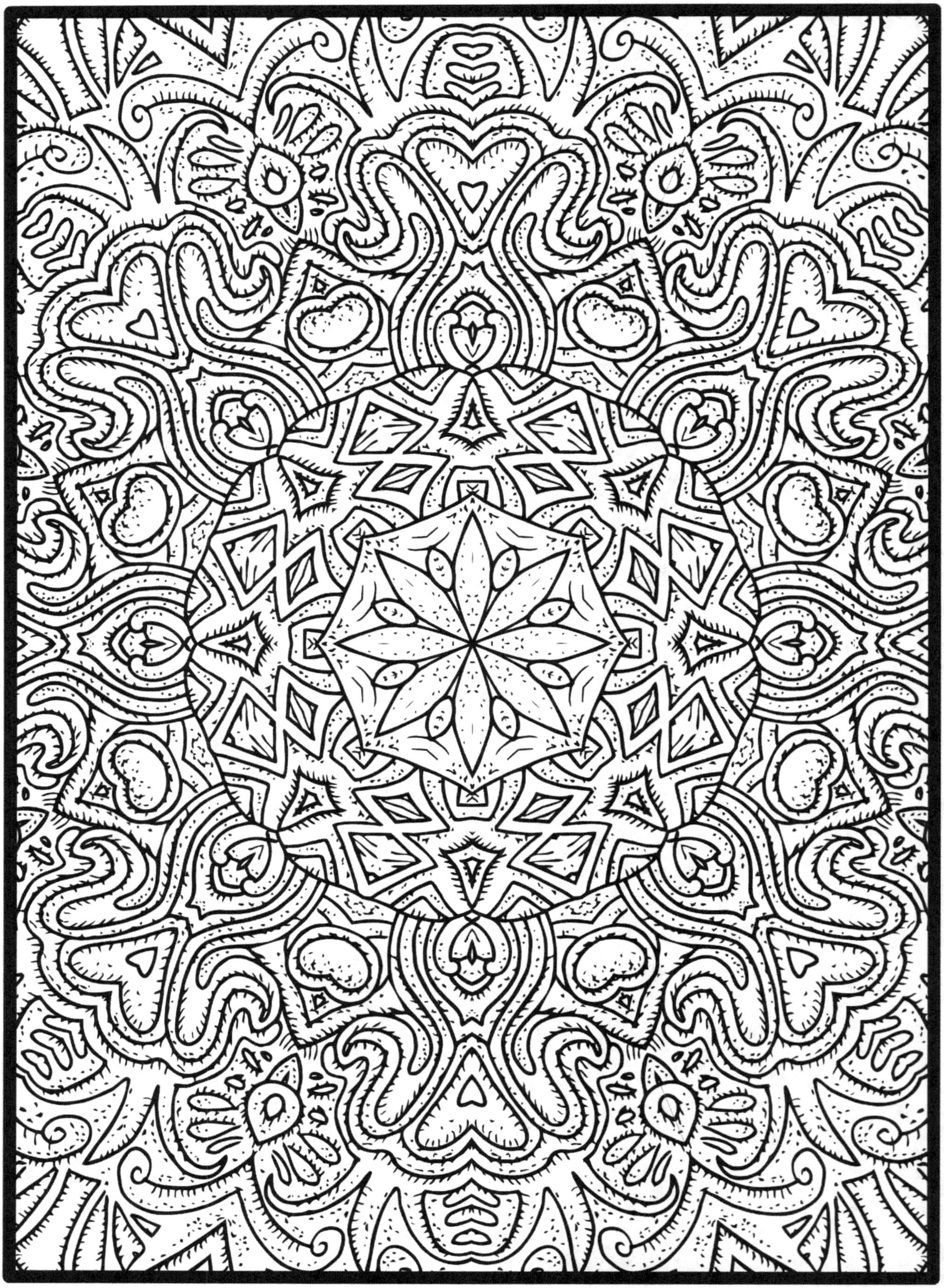

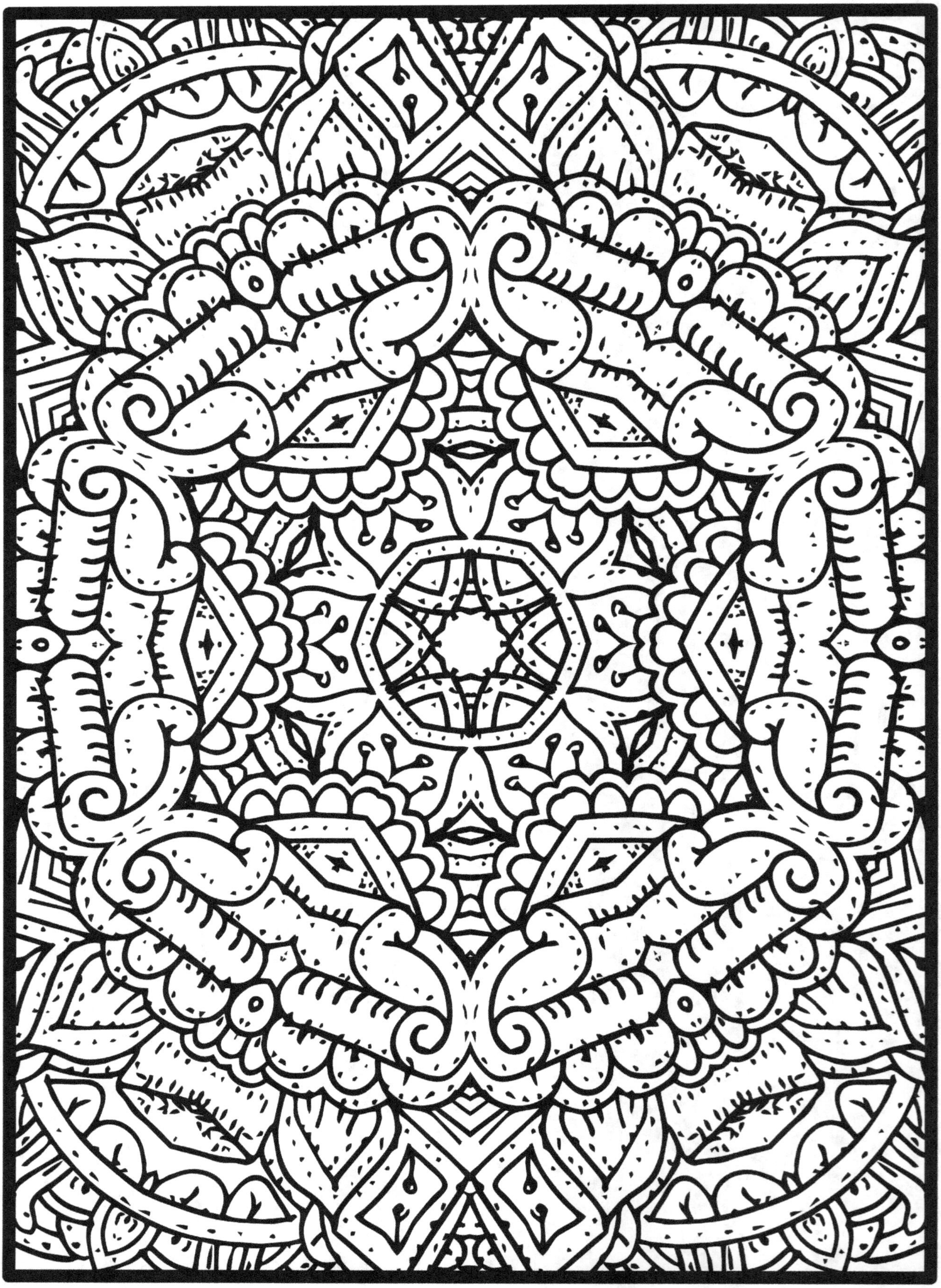

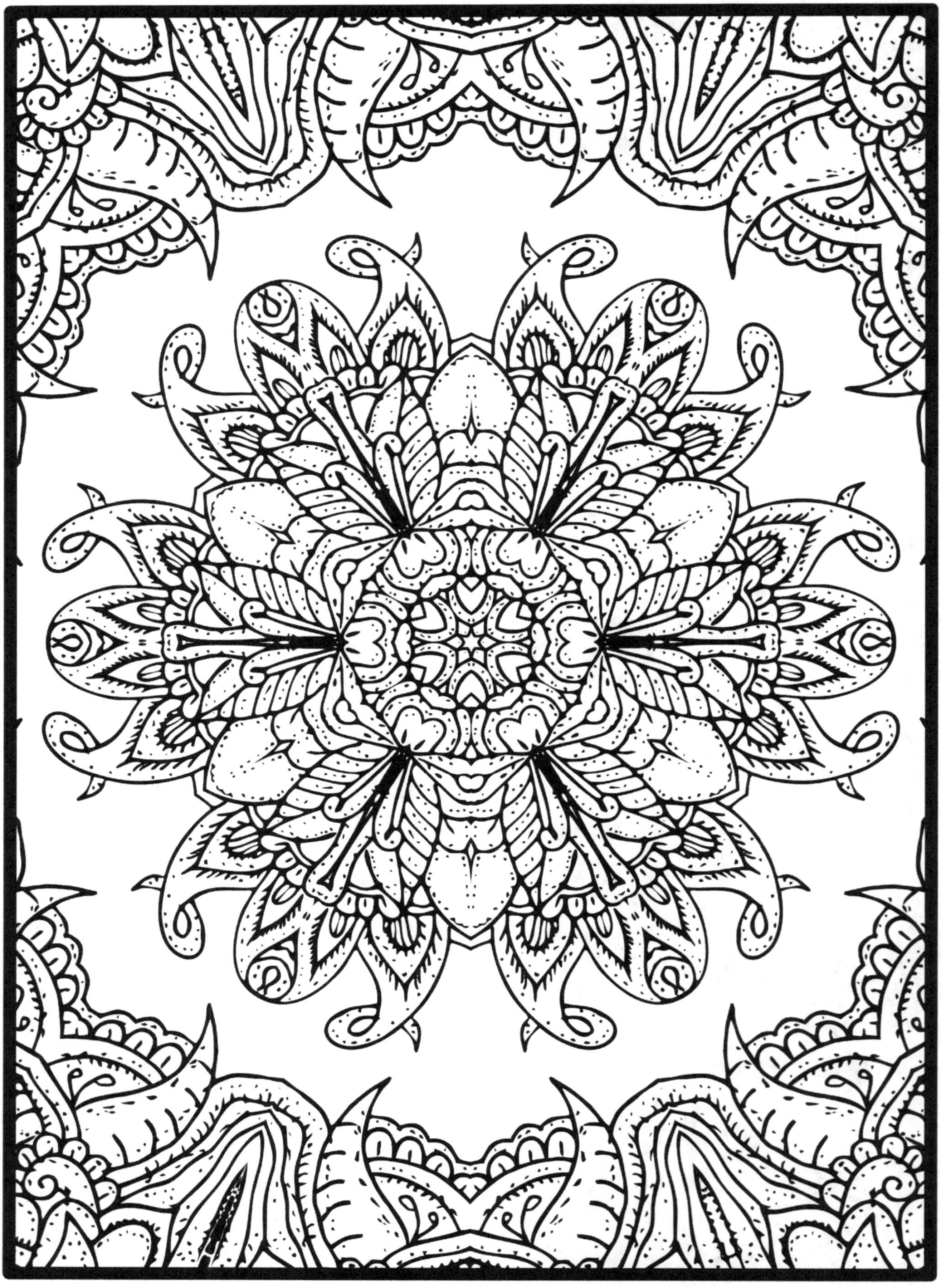

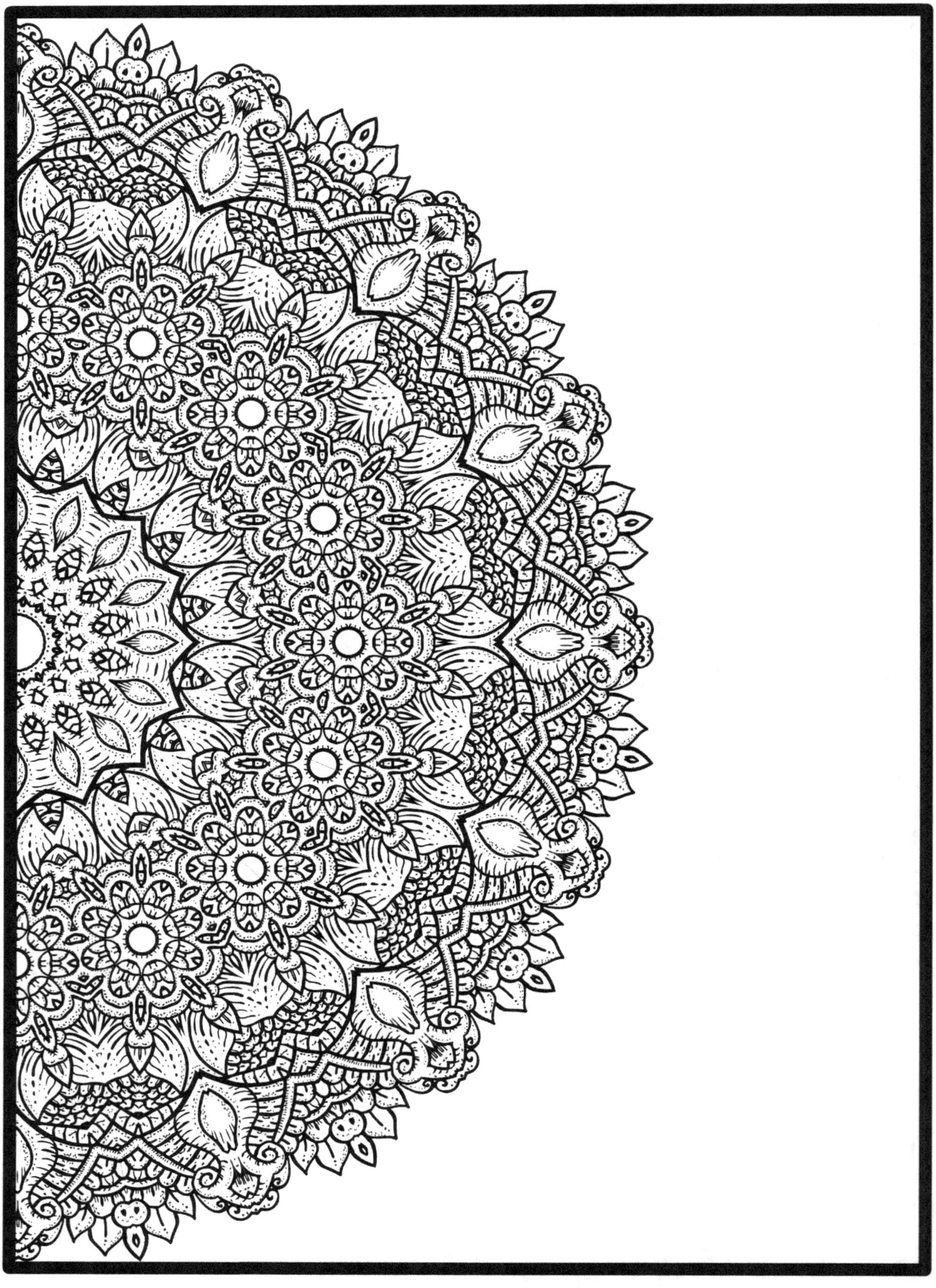

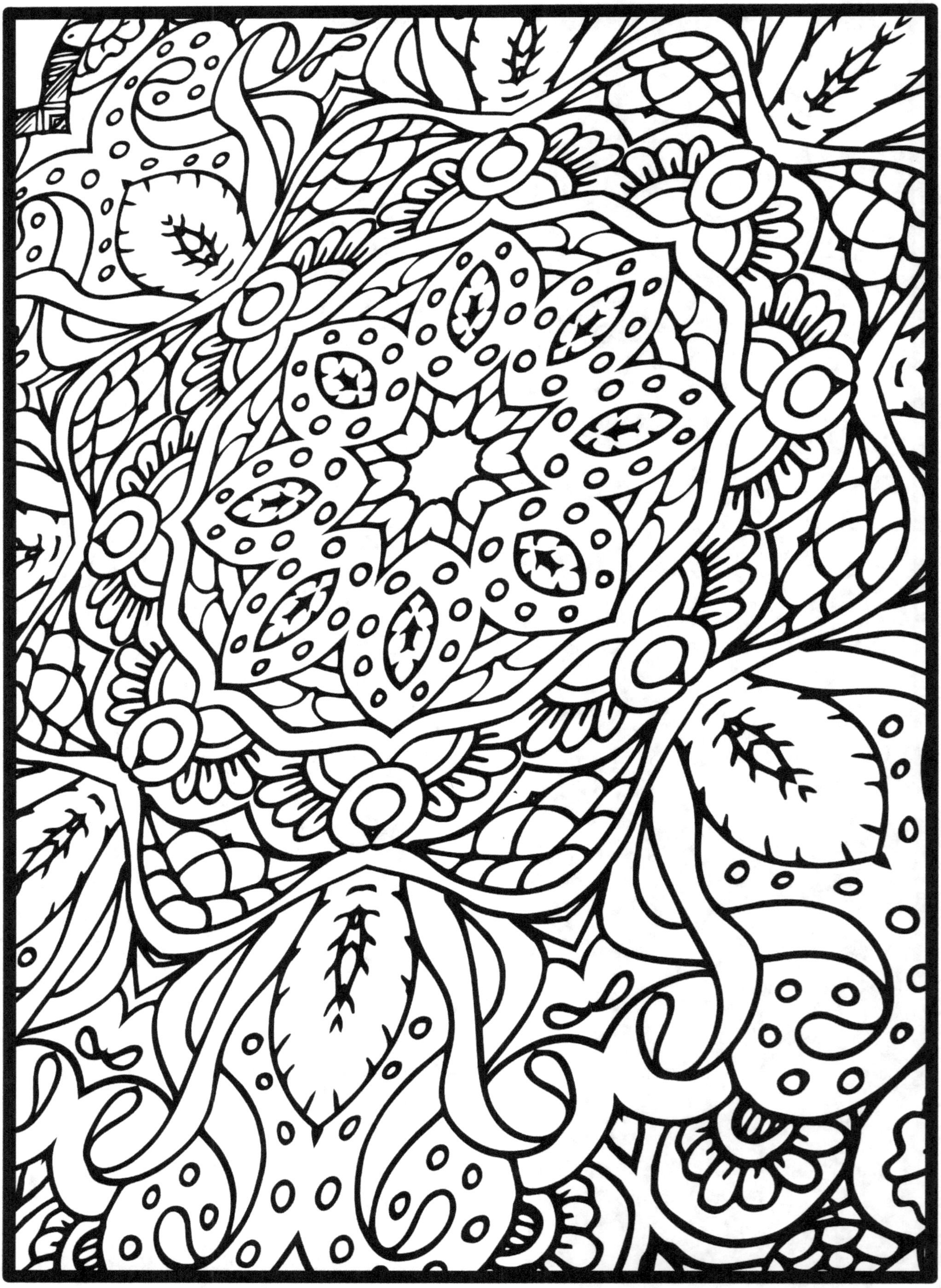

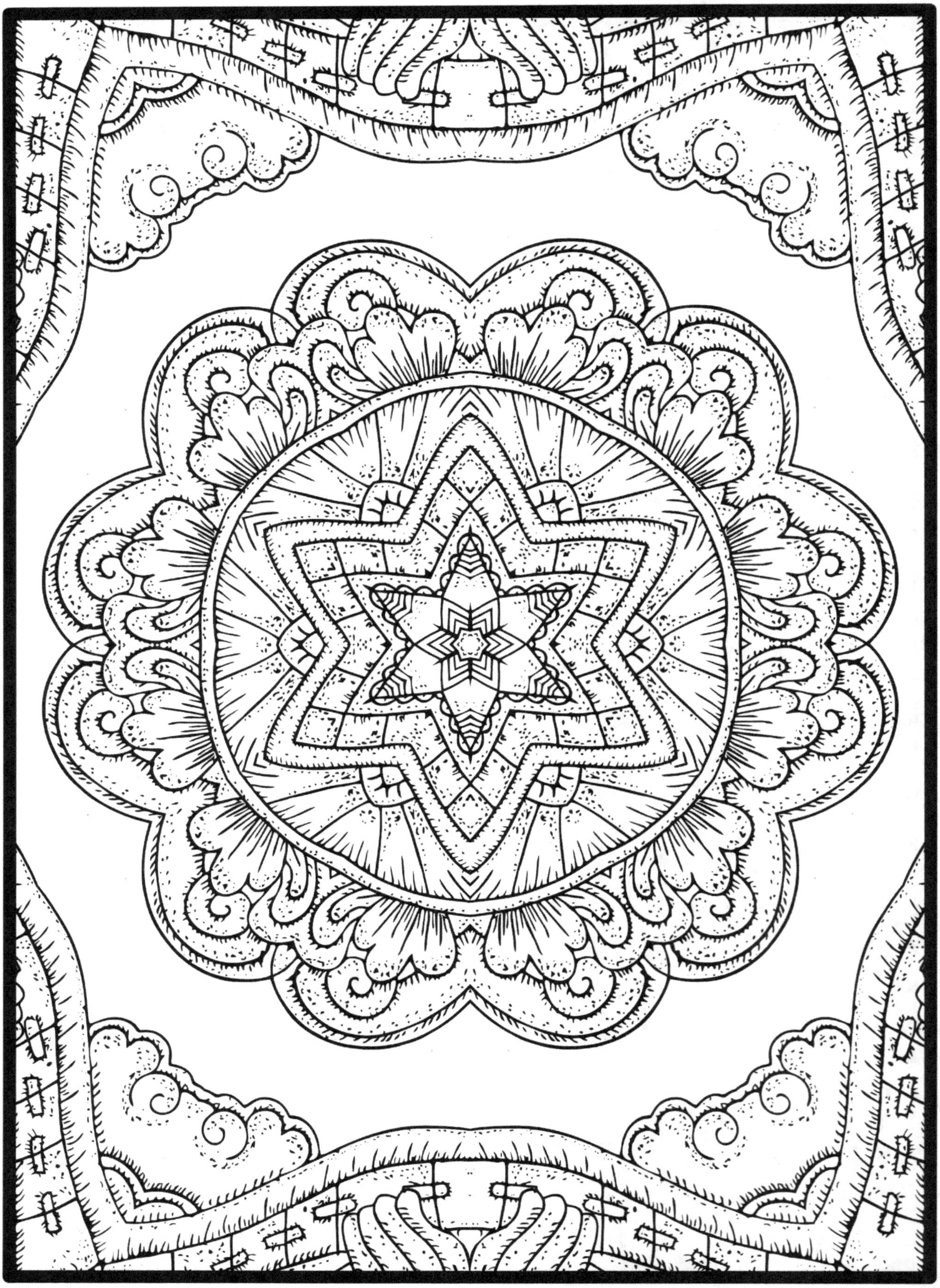

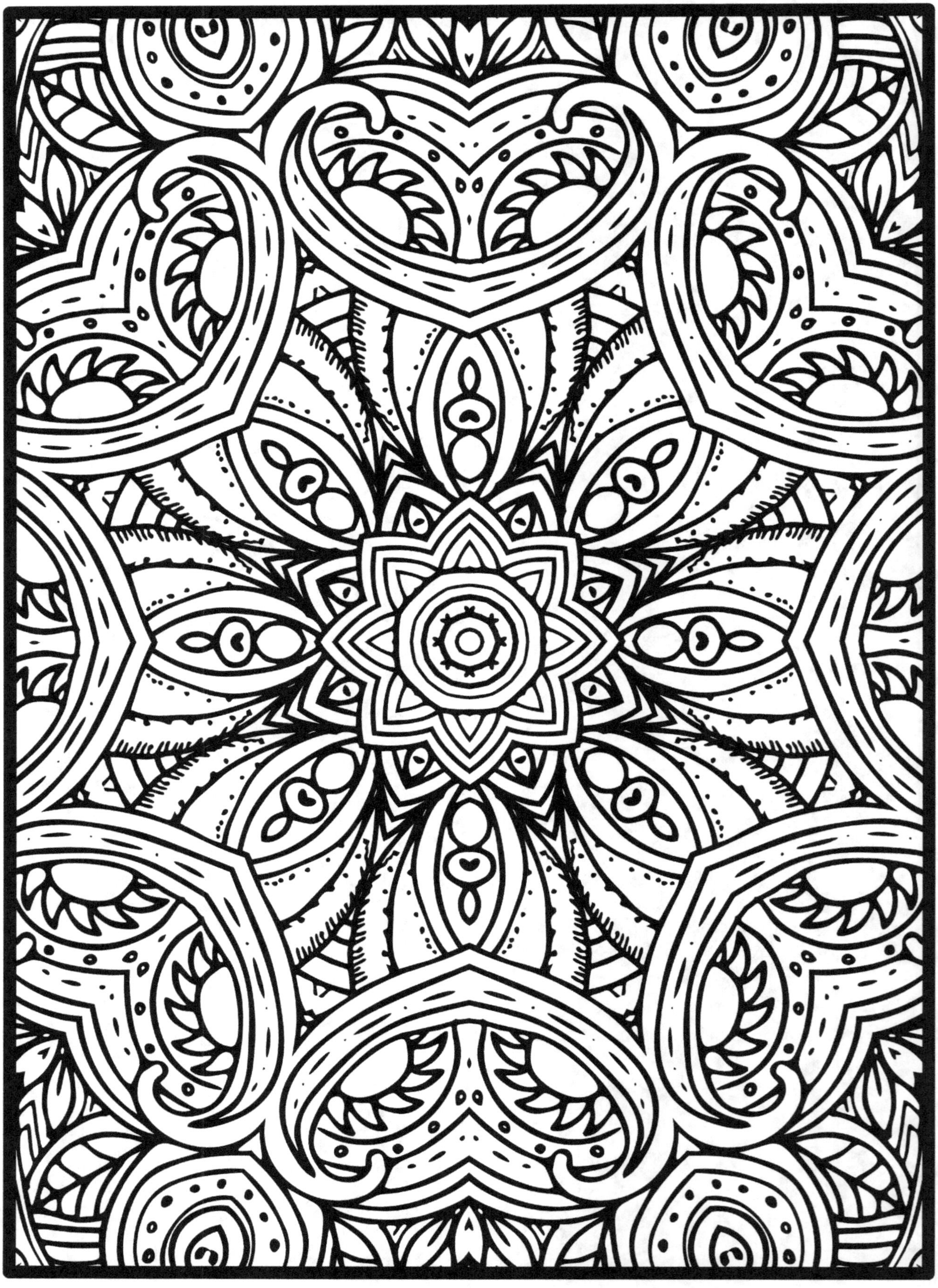

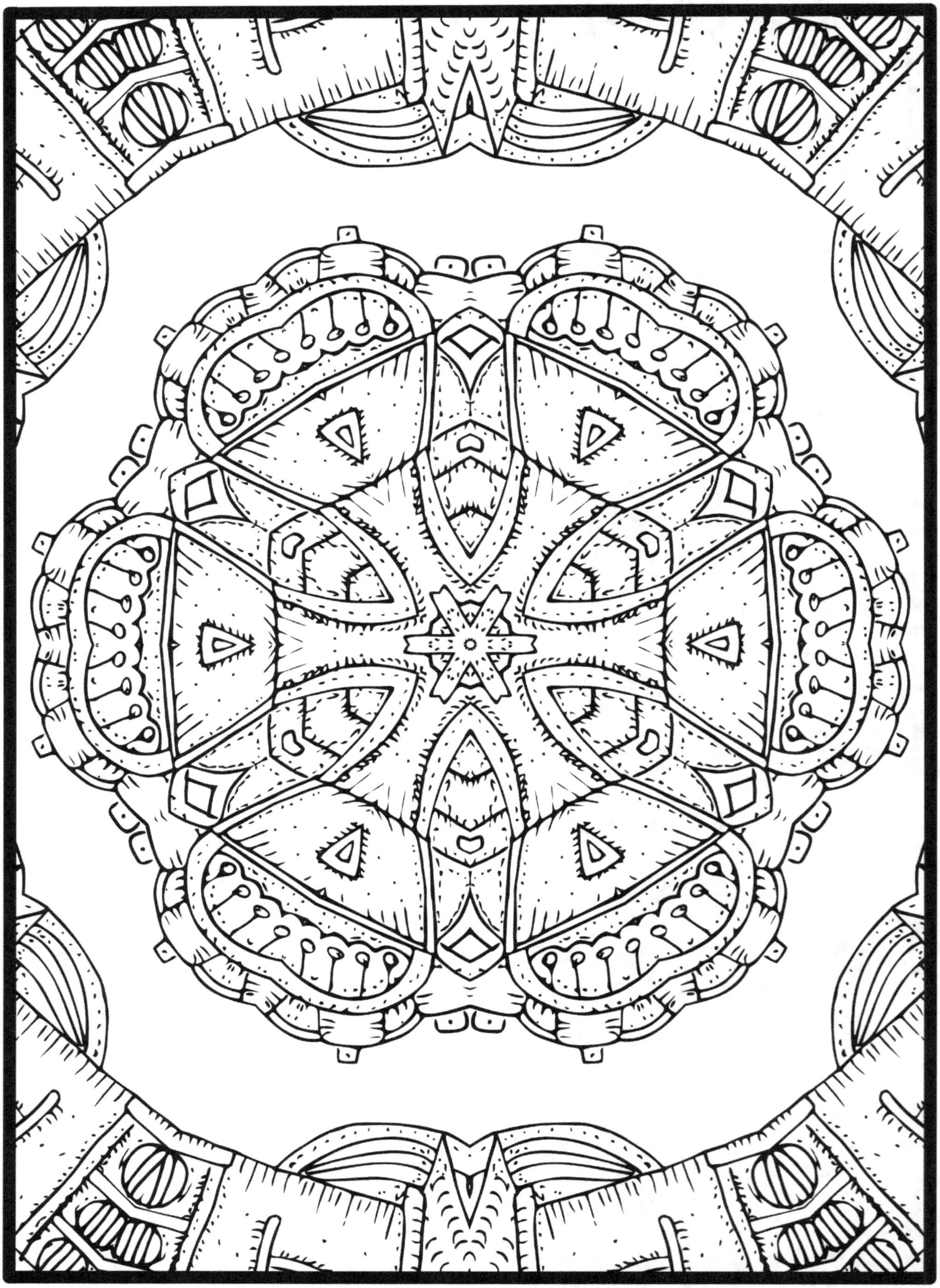

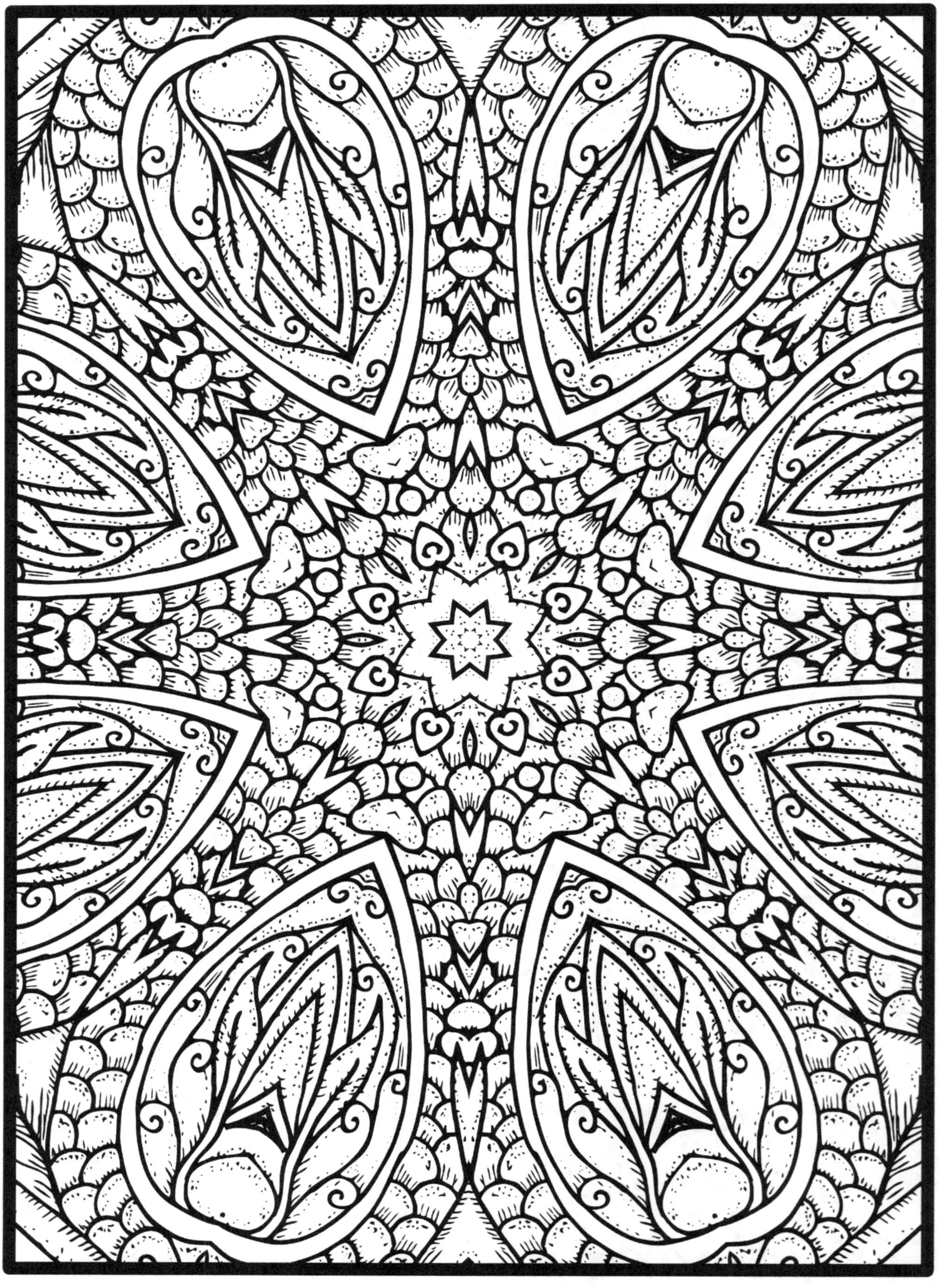

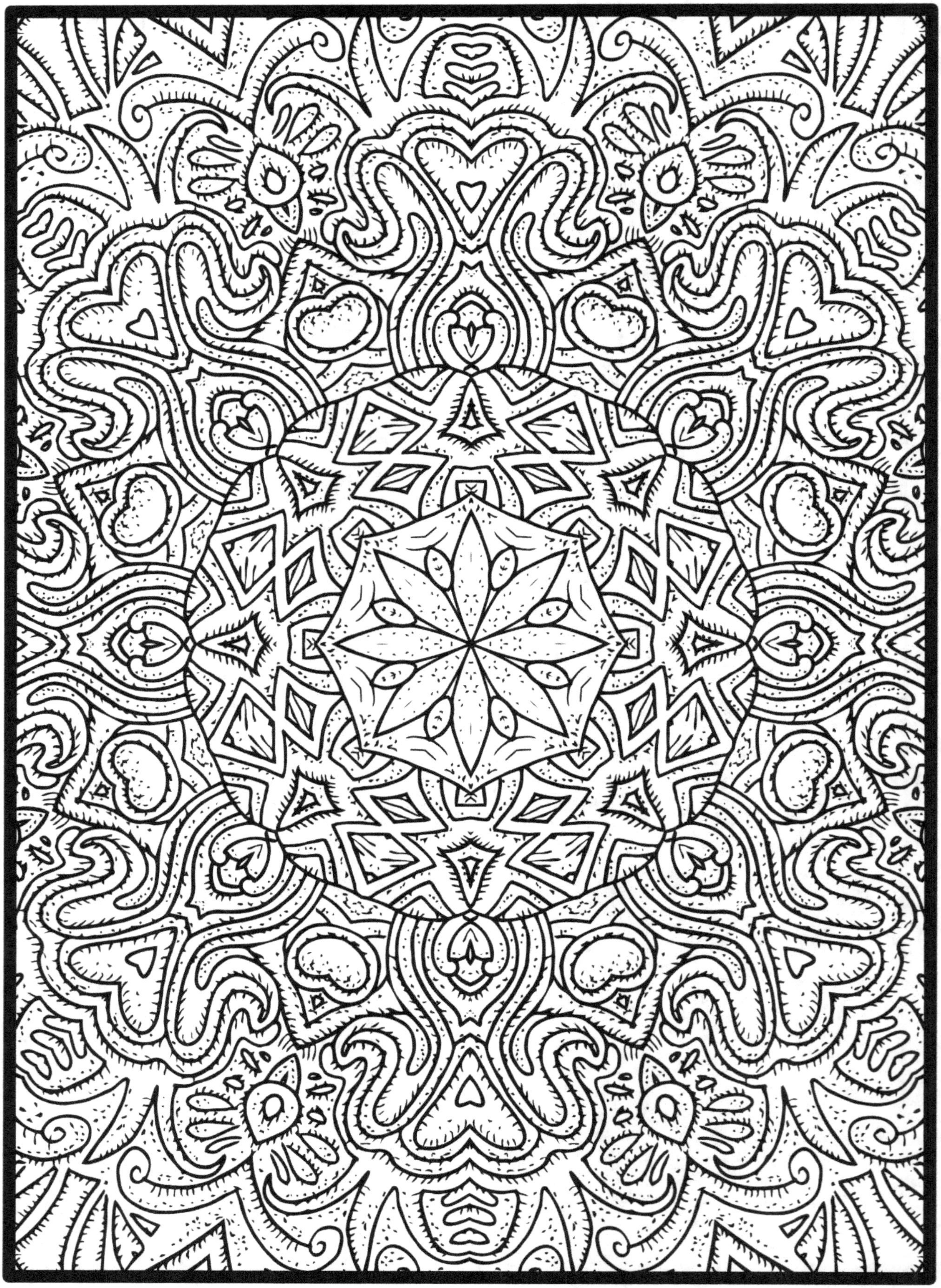

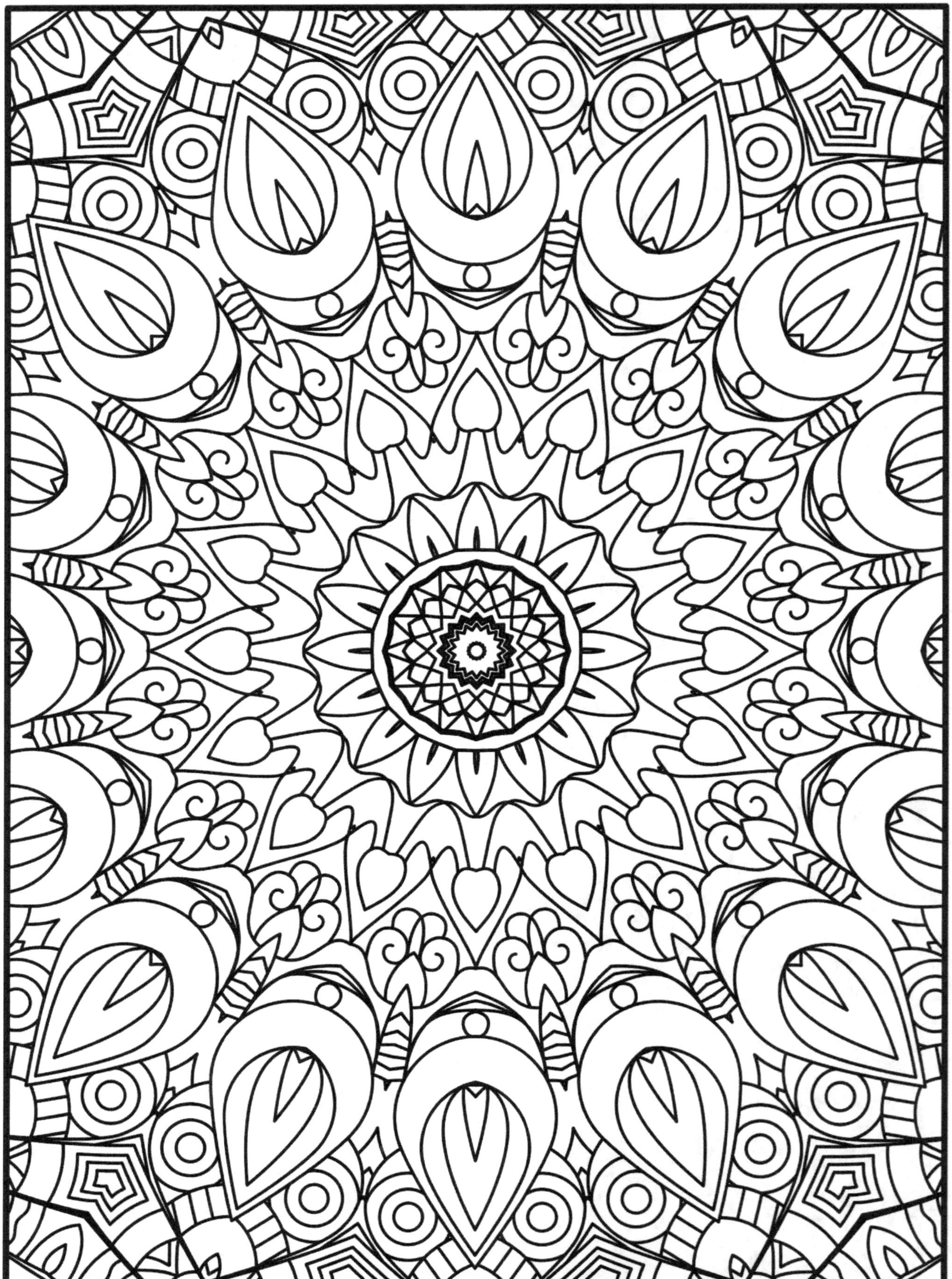